ACT I - An English Country Village.

ACT II. Madame Blum's Dressmaking Salon, Paris.

THE QUAKER GIRL

A Musical Play
in Three Acts

Book by
JAMES T. TANNER
and
EMILE LITTLER

Lyrics by
ADRIAN ROSS and PERCY GREENBANK

Music by
LIONEL MONCKTON

"THE QUAKER GIRL" was first produced at the Adelphi Theatre on 5th November, 1910 and ran for 536 performances, with a cast starring Gertie Millar and Joe Coyne. This popular success was subsequently played all over the world.

Emile Littler revised the text and revived the piece, producing it himself at the London Coliseum on 25th May, 1944. This production closed owing to flying bombs, went on tour, and later opened again in London, this time at the Stoll Theatre, in February, 1945.

"THE QUAKER GIRL" then toured England and Scotland continuously from the Summer of 1945 until December 1948, being received everywhere with the greatest enthusiasm.

This is the script of the Emile Littler presentation.

Copyright 1949 by ASSOCIATED PLAY RIGHTS LTD.

Copyright © 1949 by James T. Tanner and Emile Littler
Lyrics Copyright © 1949 by Adrian Ross and Percy Greenbank
Music Copyright © 1949 by Lionel Monckton
All Rights Reserved

THE QUAKER GIRL is fully protected under the copyright laws of the British Commonwealth, including Canada, the United States of America, and all other countries of the Copyright Union. All rights, including professional and amateur stage productions, recitation, lecturing, public reading, motion picture, radio broadcasting, television and the rights of translation into foreign languages are strictly reserved.

ISBN 978-0-573-09604-4

www.samuelfrench.co.uk
www.samuelfrench.com

For Amateur Production Enquiries

United Kingdom and World
excluding north america
plays@samuelfrench.co.uk
020 7255 4302/01

Each title is subject to availability from Samuel French,
depending upon country of performance.

CAUTION: Professional and amateur producers are hereby warned that *THE QUAKER GIRL* is subject to a licensing fee. Publication of this play does not imply availability for performance. Both amateurs and professionals considering a production are strongly advised to apply to the appropriate agent before starting rehearsals, advertising, or booking a theatre. A licensing fee must be paid whether the title is presented for charity or gain and whether or not admission is charged.

No one shall make any changes in this title for the purpose of production. No part of this book may be reproduced, stored in a retrieval system, or transmitted in any form, by any means, now known or yet to be invented, including mechanical, electronic, photocopying, recording, videotaping, or otherwise, without the prior written permission of the publisher. No one shall upload this title, or part of this title, to any social media websites.

The right of James T. Tanner and Emile Littler to be identified as authors, and Adrian Ross and Percy Greenbank as lyricists, of this work has been asserted in accordance with Section 77 of the Copyright, Designs and Patents Act 1988.

ACT III—The Pré Catalan, outside Paris.

INDEX

	PAGE
Scene Photographs	*Frontispiece*
Cast	3
Act I	5
Act II	44
Act III	79
Dance Plot	90
Ground Plans	95-97
Property Plot	98
Lighting Plot	100
Dress Plot	102

Average Playing Times:

Overture	2 Minutes
Act I	57 ,,
Interval	10 ,,
Act II	56 ,,
Interval	9 ,,
Act III	23 ,,
TOTAL	2 Hours, 37 Minutes

SYNOPSIS OF SCENES

ACT I.   An English Country Village.
         (*Average Playing Time* : *57 mins.*)

ACT II. Madame Blum's Dressmaking Salon, Paris.
         (*Average Playing Time* : *56 mins.*)

ACT III. The Pré Catalan, Outside Paris.
         (*Average Playing Time* : *23 mins.*)

Time : Not the Present.

CHARACTERS

In the Order of their Appearance	Played in Revival by:
JARGE, Village Crier and Church Clerk	DIMITRI VETTER
MRS. LUKYN, Landlady of " The Chequers " Inn	MARCELLE TURNER
WILLIAM, Waiter at " The Chequers "	WILLIAM HENRY
NATHANIEL PYM, A Quaker	DEWEY GIBSON
RACHEL, His Sister	LUCILLE DALE
PHOEBE, An English Maid to Princess Mathilde	APRIL ROSS
CAPTAIN CHARTERIS, A King's Messenger	PAT MCGRATH
PRINCESS MATHILDE, An Exiled Bonapartist	JOY HAYDEN
MADAME BLUM, Proprietress of " La Maison Blum," Paris	IVY ST. HELIER
TONY CHUTE, Naval Attache at the American Embassy, Paris	BILLY MILTON
JEREMIAH, A Quaker. Servant to Nathaniel	HAL BRYAN
PRUDENCE PYM, A Quakeress. Niece to Nathaniel	CELIA LIPTON
TOINETTE, Head Fitter at " La Maison Blum "	JASMINE DEE
MONSIEUR LAROSE, Parisian Chief of Police	DIMITRI VETTER
DIANE, A Parisian Actress	PEGGY LIVESEY
PRINCE CARLO, Affianced to Princess Mathilde	GEOFFREY DUNN
MONSIEUR DUHAMEL, A Minister of State	STANLEY DREWITT
PRINCIPAL DANCER	PAMELA FOSTER

The Chorus of the Revival consists of :
Male and Female Villagers ; 8 Quakers ; 6 Quakeresses, in Act I.

6 Mannequins ; 8 Work Girls ; 20 Lady Racing Guests ; 12 Racing Men ; 2 Pages ; 2 Gendarmes, in Act II.

Ladies and Gentlemen as Guests of Prince Carlo, 8 " Couleur de Rose " Dancers, 6 Wine Waiters, in Act III.

THE QUAKER GIRL

ACT I

(ALL VILLAGERS *on stage at rise of Curtain.* JARGE *discovered C.* MRS. LUKYN *at Inn door. For movements see Dance Plot.*)

No. 1.—OPENING CHORUS and SOLO :—(MRS. LUKYN).

CHORUS :
    Jarge, we've such a tale to tell
      Have you heard about it ?
    There's a lady, quite a swell
      Nobody can doubt it !
    She arrived a week ago,
      Staying at the Chequers,
    With a dozen trunks or so,
      Regular three deckers !

(JARGE *stands C., surrounded by* GIRLS.)

(JARGE *is uninterested.*)

    True it is, you may depend,
      Prudence Pym, the Quaker—
    She's the foreign lady's friend
      Never will forsake her.
    Goes to see her every day,
      Nobody can stop her,
    Though the other Quakers say
      That it isn't proper !

(FULL CHORUS *turn facing door of Inn L., looking at* Mrs. LUKYN.)

1st VILLAGER : There's Mrs. Lukyn at " The Chequers " door !
2nd VILLAGER : She is the party who can tell us more.
3rd VILLAGER : She's so obliging she will not refuse !
CHORUS : Here, Mrs. Lukyn, have you any news ?

(MRS. LUKYN *comes to C. with arms folded, walking in time to music.* JARGE *on her R.* GIRLS *cluster round her.*)

MRS. LUKYN :
    I am not the sort to chatter
      Though I'm fairly young.
CHORUS :
    So thinks each man !
MRS. LUKYN :
    On a most important matter
      I can hold my tongue !
CHORUS :
    No doubt you can !
MRS. LUKYN :
    So if I should tell you something
      Heard I won't say whence
CHORUS :
    Of course we know !
MRS. LUKYN :
    You'll be silent as a dumb thing
      It's in confidence !
CHORUS :
    Just so !

(NOTE :—*These lines can be omitted if desired.*)

Mrs. Lukyn:	Gossips are all mischief makers, Slyly whispering—
Chorus:	Yes, that's too true. (*Nodding in time to music*).
Mrs. Lukyn:	You must be as mum as Quakers, Don't repeat a thing!
Chorus:	That we won't do.
Mrs. Lukyn:	I have always hated scandal With a scorn intense (*She lifts hands up in mock horror*).
Chorus:	Quite right, we know!
Mrs. Lukyn:	So whatever now I handle, Is in confidence!
Chorus:	Just so!
Mrs. Lukyn:	(*C.*) Now, what do you want to know? (*Looking to L. and R. as all gossips do*).
Chorus:	Is the lady here a Queen? (*Confidentially*). Has she got a lover? Tell us all that you have seen, All you can discover! Has she rashly run away From a husband jealous? Is she single, can you say? Tell us—only tell us! Tell us all the news! (Mrs. Lukyn *shakes her head and turns to go into Inn, the* Chorus *again protest—and keep her C.*)
Mrs. Lukyn:	(*C.*) Now it's no use asking me, I never talk about my customers. (All *Laugh*).
Mrs. Lukyn:	All I know is that the young lady staying at my Hotel—(*There is amusement, at the word "Hotel."*)—be a lady if ever there was one, for all she's French. Here, you Jim, you (*to* Ostler Boy *R.C.*) go and help Jobson get the shay ready to meet the 10.45.
Jim:	Aye, aye, mum. (*Exit* Ostler Boy *L.3.*) (Mrs. Lukyn *C. Interest amongst the* Villagers.) (*At this point a few* Villagers *exit R.U.E. and L.U.E.*).
Jarge:	(*R.C.*) More arrivals, Mrs. Lukyn, mum? (*Hand to ear*).
Mrs. Lukyn:	Friends of the young lady, Jarge—she told me she was expecting 'em.
Jarge:	(*R.*) And Phoebe—the postman's darter—be her maid now? She'll be a furriner herself soon an' speakin' accordin', for sure! (*C.*) (*More* Villagers *Exit L.U.E.*).

Mrs. LUKYN :	Phoebe be a good girl, Master Jarge. Tho' given to gossip. (*R.*) And when the young lady asked me if I knew any nice girl— (WILLIAM *Enters from Inn*). —she could engage, I thought of Phoebe. (*Sneeze from* WILLIAM *Goes L.*) William ! (*The remaining* VILLAGERS *Exit L. and R.U.E.*).
WILLIAM :	(*L.C.*) Ah, that be the pepper ! The moth do nesty so in these dress things. (*The stage is clear of* VILLAGERS *by now*).
Mrs. LUKYN :	For goodness' sake, William, don't go near the young lady till you've given yourself a good shake. (*She moves over to* WILLIAM *and brushes him*).
WILLIAM :	(*L.C.*) Lor' ! The young lady and that gal Phoebe be so excited they don't take no notice of pepper. First it's Phoebe—" William, has the train arrived yet "—and then it's the young lady—" But where is the 10.45." (JARGE *C., very interested, with hand to ear*).
Mrs. LUKYN :	Bless my heart ! It ain't ten yet.
WILLIAM :	(*Crosses in front of* Mrs. LUKYN *to C.*) Oh ! and Missis ! She've ordered breakfast.
Mrs. LUKYN :	Breakfast, William ?
WILLIAM :	At twelve o'clock, she says dejunay—that's French for the 10.45, I s'pose. Oh ! and she says "wine for the gentlemen."
Mrs. LUKYN :	(*Crosses L.*) Breakfast at twelve ! Gentlemen ! Wine ! (*Goes up to Inn door*) Oh, I must go and see what it's all about ! (*Exits*).
JARGE :	I've got it—for sure—it's a runaway match. (JARGE *R.C. and* WILLIAM *L.C. sit on seat at tree. Music proceeds from 5th bar.*)

No. 2.—QUAKER CHORUS AND ENSEMBLE
" Quakers Meeting "

(*Enter the* QUAKER *Community from R.I.E. The males and females are strictly separated. All carry prayer-books, hands in front of them.* GIRLS *Enter first, in single-file, followed by* MEN. *They form two lines across stage,* GIRLS *in front line. See Dance Plot.*).

QUAKERS : While our worthy village neighbours
　　Gossip, or resume their labours,
From the busy world retreating,
　　We will hold our Quakers' meeting. (*All bob and bow*)
With our friends and our relations
　　Sit in silent meditations, (*All bow heads*)
Not a single word repeating—
　　So we hold our Quakers' meeting !

QUAKERS *cross* R. *and form 2 lines up and down stage—*
(*Enter* VILLAGE GIRLS *and* MEN *from all sides except down stage* R. *See Dance Plot*).

VILLAGE GIRLS : Why are you looking so glum and blue,
    Solomon, Solomon Grundy?
We have a budget of news for you,
    Solomon, Solomon Grundy!

VILLAGE MEN : (*Coming forward*)
There have been such goings on at the Inn,
Really we hardly know where to begin.
Stay for a chat—for it isn't a sin,
    Solomon, Solomon Grundy!

VILLAGE GIRLS : Ah! Why should you stick in your hall all day,
    Solomon, Solomon Grundy?
Passing the time in a foolish way,
Nothing to drink nor a word to say!
    Solomon, Solomon Grundy

VILLAGE MEN : Couldn't you leave it till Sunday?

ALL VILLAGERS : Stay and be wise,
Open your eyes,
    Solomon, Solomon Grundy!

(QUAKERS *walk four paces forward—and four paces back.*)

QUAKERS : Nay, friends—nay.
Nay, friends—nay—we cannot stay.

(QUAKERS *walk in time with the music in single file of* MEN *and* GIRLS—*the upstage* MAN *and* GIRL *leading, followed by the others—so that at the end of "to our meeting" they have completed a complete circle. They form up in two lines,* GIRLS *in front,* MEN *behind—downstage, as on their first entrance. This time they only stretch across the front of the stage to* L. C.—*as the* VILLAGERS *occupy the* L. *side of the stage.*)

ENSEMBLE

VILLAGERS	QUAKERS
Don't be as mum as any mouse	Tho' your gossip and your chatter
When the cat is at her,	May not be a sinful matter,
Leave your stuffy meeting-house	
That'll never matter!	
We've a lot of news to tell	Wordly pleasures are but fleeting
That'll take some beating;	
So today you might as well	We prefer a Quakers' meeting!
Drop your Quakers' meeting!	

	Have a talk and take a glass We will wish you all
	That'll be enjoyment ; enjoyment
	If you want the time to pass In your profitless
	That's the right employ- employment,
	ment !
	Stay a bit and you will And withdraw with
	hear friendly greeting,
	Something worth repeating, To our quiet Quakers'
	Then we'll leave you, meeting !
	never fear Our quiet meeting—
	To your Quakers' meeting ! To our meeting !
	(*During the last 5 bars of Number*, NATHANIEL *and* RACHEL *to C. R. They are brother and sister, alike in appearance, and are the heads of the Quakers. Two lines up and down stage in front of cottage R.*)
NATHANIEL :	(*R.C.*) Friends ! Why doth thy footsteps falter on the way? (RACHEL *on his R., moving to R.C.*).
JARGE :	(*C.*) Why, Master Pym, being neighbours, we thought you'd like to hear the news. (*Moves up C.*).
WILLIAM :	(*to L.C.*) Mr. Nathaniel, the young lady in the hotel be asking to see your niece, Miss Prudence.
NATHANIEL :	Say unto the foreign maiden that our niece is even now wrestling with the flesh in the meeting house yonder. (*Indicating meeting house offstage R.*)
WILLIAM :	Why, you ain't been and shut Miss Prudence up on a beautiful June morning like this, have you ?
NATHANIEL :	She hath been secluded from contamination, friend.
RACHEL :	Come, friends, the spirit may move us to further admonish our erring niece.
	MUSIC CUE : No. 2½.—EXIT OF QUAKERS
	(QUAKERS *Exit R.U.E. in pairs, followed by* NATHANIEL *and* RACHEL).
JARGE :	(*Crossing to R.C.*) Drives yon Quaker lass too hard they do.
WILLIAM :	(*C.*) I often say as she'll take the bit between her teeth some day.
	(*Enter* PHOEBE *from Inn. She is a village girl, but full of the importance of her new position— and putting on a bit of " side "—she speaks with country dialect*).
PHOEBE :	(*L.C., with a busy air*) Oh, William, have 'ee ordered the dejunay ? (*Crosses R.*)
WILLIAM :	They be getting the shay ready now to meet it.
PHOEBE :	Ah ! I be forgetting 'ee don't speak French, William. Dejunay is French. (*Moves to C. between* WILLIAM *and* JARGE).
JARGE :	(*R.C.*) Ah, what *be* dejunay, Phoebe ?

PHOEBE : (*Moves to R.C. with an air of propriety*). Never you mind ! There be some things as no gentleman mentions to a lady.
(*During this* WILLIAM *and* JARGE, *who moves to L. C. to* WILLIAM, *are tickled by airs* PHOEBE *gives herself.*)

WILLIAM : How do 'ee like your new place, Phoebe ?

PHOEBE : (*With a more natural manner*). Oh, she be a dear, be mamselle.

WILLIAM : (*L.C. and* JARGE *R.*) Mamselle ? And what might that be French for ?

PHOEBE : (*Glibly*) That be French for Princess. (*Suddenly stops and recollects herself*).
(JARGE *and* WILLIAM *stare in amazement at the word " Princess," they betray great anxiety to spread the news.*)

JARGE : Princess ! Princess ! Here, Willum ! (*Picks up bell from seat C.*) I want to run down to the village.—(*U/L.*)

WILLIAM : Princess ! (*Breathlessly*). Where be Mrs. Lukyn ? (*Exits through Inn door*).

PHOEBE : (*In agitation*) Oh, now I've done it. (*Runs to stage L. and then crosses R.*) They old wag-tongues'll spread it all over the village.
(*Enter* MATHILDE *from Inn, L. She is a charming girl of about twenty, simply dressed in a pretty summer frock. She is quite English in manner, and only in one or two little peculiarities of phrasing betrays her foreign birth. She places her hat on L. up stage side of tree C.*).

MATHILDE : (*L., who is eager and expectant in manner*) Oh, Phoebe, hasn't the train arrived yet ?

PHOEBE : (*R.*) No, your Highness. (*Curtseys. Claps her hand to her mouth*) Oh—(*Bus.*)

MATHILDE : (*Holding up a warning finger with a smile*) Phoebe, you must forget I told you all that. (*She moves to L.C. stage*).

PHOEBE : Oh ! I be that sorry, your Highness—(*Curtsey*)—I mean miss—mamselle—you ain't going to send me away—because I made that little mistake ? Are you ?
(*During this speech* PHOEBE *becomes more confused and agitated*).

MATHILDE : No—no—of course not— (*Moves to L. of stage*). If you like, you shall stay with me after I am married.

PHOEBE : Married ! Mamselle—miss—what, here—in the village—today ?

MATHILDE : (*Nods*) Today ! (*Moves to C.*). Yes, Phoebe ! I am to be married today. (*Happily*) Not to the husband they chose for me, in France, but to one I have chosen for myself. It's a secret. You see, I have run away from school at Cheltenham. (*Sits on bench in front of tree*).

PHOEBE : (*Comes down to R.C.*) School ? A big grown girl like you, mamselle ? Be you backward then ? (MATHILDE *laughs.*) And is that your young man who be a-coming by the 10.45 ? (*Pointing off stage R.*)

MATHILDE : Phoebe—*please* say, Captain Charteris. He's a King's Messenger, the best, the *dearest* man in all the world.

PHOEBE : So he ought to be, to marry you, miss.

MATHILDE : Tell me, haven't *you* a sweetheart ?

PHOEBE : (*Playing with corner of her apron*) Well, off and on so to speak. (*Break slight R.*)

MATHILDE : Off and on—oh, but that's terrible.

PHOEBE : Just what I say, but it ain't my fault.

MATHILDE : Who is it ?

PHOEBE : Jeremiah, the Quakers' man-servant, over there. (*Looks and points off stage R. to Quakers' door*). He be a blow-hot and blow-cold 'un, he be.

MATHILDE : Blow-hot and blow-cold 'un ? (*In mock bewilderment*).

PHOEBE : Yes, mamselle. Some days he be like wild horses, fair scarrifying to a proper minded maid he be—other days he be that backward—(*Kicks foot unhappily*)

MATHILDE : (*Rises from bench, crosses R.*) Oh, but Phoebe, we're talking here and the train may have arrived. Do go to the station and see. (*Pushes* PHOEBE *up stage, R. follows her U/S.*)

PHOEBE : Yes, mamselle. (*Going R. and returning*) How will I know Captain——?

MATHILDE : Charteris. You couldn't mistake him anywhere.

PHOEBE : All right, miss. Only it would never do to bring you the wrong one. (*Exits upstage R.*).

No. 3.—SONG : (MATHILDE)
" O Time, Time "
(*For Movements see Dance Plot*)

MATHILDE : While I'm waiting here in eager expectation,
  Gladly watching for my lover to appear,

(*Sits on seat in front of tree*)
In my fanciful and fond imagination
  Ev'ry moment seems a year.

(*Gets up from seat, and walks L.*)
All impatient, from the break of day till sundown,
  I keep wishing that the hours were not so long ;
For it seems to me that ev'ry watch has run down,
  And that all the clocks are wrong—

(*Rises*)
O, Time Time !
　You are really most unkind.
　Why is it you're inclined
　To lag so far behind ?　(*Moves D/C.*)
　　You may go
　　Slow.
　When we meet, my love and I, (*Moves L.*)
　But till then I want the time, I want the time to fly !

(*Moves over to R.*)
To and fro in anxious mood I can't help pacing,
　I can turn my thoughts to nothing else but this—
How I wish my love and I were now embracing,
　How I'm longing for his kiss.

(*Moves C.*)
So at ev'ry sound my heart goes beating madly,
　As I listen for his footsteps at the gate ;
Then I hear the village chime, and murmur sadly—
　" There's another hour to wait ! "

(*Moves over to L.*)
Oh, Time, Time !
　You are really most unkind.
　Why is it you're inclined
　To lag so far behind ?
　　You may go—(*To C.*)
　　Slow.
　When we meet, my love and I,
　But till then I want the time, I want the time to fly !
　　Fly away, Time !　Fly away, Time !
　　Fly away, Time !　Fly away !

(MATHILDE *finishes L.C., in curtsey.*)

(*Enter* PHOEBE *excitedly—R.U.E.*)

PHOEBE :	(*C.*) Miss, miss, the train's come in, miss.
MATHILDE :	(*L.*) Has—hasn't Captain Charteris come by it ? (*Agitated*).
PHOEBE :	There be two gentlemen, miss. One of them chucked me under the chin.—(*Crosses L.*)
MATHILDE :	That couldn't possibly be Captain Charteris, Phoebe !
PHOEBE :	Ah ! Then it must be the other.

(*Enter* CAPTAIN CHARTERIS *from R. up stage. He comes to C. placing hat, stick and briefcase on seat R.C. where* MATHILDE *meets him.*)

CHARTERIS :	Mathilde, darling !
MATHILDE :	Brian dearest !

(CHARTERIS *and* MATHILDE *embrace, R.C.*

PHOEBE :	Oh, that must be the right one.

(*Exits into Inn as* CHARTERIS *and* MATHILDE *come down C. together.*)

No. 4.—DUET : (MATHILDE and CHARTERIS)
"Wonderful"
(*For Movements see Dance Plot*)

CHARTERIS : (*C.*) Oh my beautiful bride,
I have flown to your side,
None could stay me, or delay me—
Nobody tried !

MATHILDE : Oh, my darling, my dear, (*Break L.*)
So at last you are here !
Ev'ry second I've reckoned
Long as a year !

BOTH : Now the wedding bells may chime (*Together C.*)
As soon as they can,
For the train came in on time
According to plan.
Oh ! It can never happen again,
That was quite the most wonderful train
Since the wonderful, wonderful world began,
The world began !

CHARTERIS : I have come for my Princess (*Crosses R.*)
By the Calais boat express,
As it thundered on uproarious.

MATHILDE : (*Enthusiastically*)
That is simply glorious !

CHARTERIS : Like a nectar draught to me
Was the cup of Dover tea
And the food was rapture edible—

MATHILDE : (*Wondering*)
That is quite incredible !

CHARTERIS : There was not a moment's loss
When I got to Charing Cross
For the porters all were dutiful

MATHILDE : (*Delighted*)
Oh they must be beautiful !

CHARTERIS : (*Produces Licence*) (*Together C.*)
And the wax is red and warm
On the special licence form
And our names are written under full—
(*Puts Licence back into inside pocket*)

MATHILDE : (*Overcome*)
Oh, it's all so wonderful,
Wonderful ! Wonderful ! Wonderful !

CHARTERIS : Now the sky is serene.
None can now intervene,
None can sever us for ever,
You are my Queen !

MATHILDE :	I'll be married to you
	In a minute or two,
	   It is dazing and amazing,
	   Can it be true ?

BOTH :	Let the curate robe in white
	   As soon as he can,
	And in holy wedlock plight
	   The woman and man !
	Oh (*you*), give (*me*) a kiss and a ring,
	   (*I*) (*you*)
	It is quite the most wonderful thing
	   Since the wonderful world began.

MATHILDE :	(*Walking R., reads*) Mathilde, Amelie, Sophie, Augusta Murat—(*Laughs*).
CHARTERIS :	Princess of France.
	(MATHILDE, *walking to* CHARTERIS *R.C., puts licence back into his inside pocket. Moves in to C. and kisses* CHARTERIS)
MATHILDE :	But when I am (*Hesitates slightly*) Mrs. Charteris— I shan't be a Prinicess any more. (*To him*)
CHARTERIS :	You will always be my Princess. (*Takes* MATHILDE'S *hands*). But how did you manage to get away from the school ? Over the garden wall ?
MATHILDE :	Oh no ! Through the garden gate. (*Moves to L.C.*) Then I came here, just as you told me.
CHARTERIS :	Yes. To marry a poor devil of an Englishman, when you might have been the wife of Prince Carlo.
MATHILDE :	Ah, but you see I want the "poor Englishman," darling and I don't want Prince Carlo. (*Sits on seat in front of tree ;* CHARTERIS *moves up with her and sits on her R.*) Now, tell me, did you see Madam Blum while you were in Paris ?
CHARTERIS :	*See* Madam Blum, darling ! Why I've half lived at the Maison Blum on purpose to talk about you. You know it's the most " chic " dressmaking place in Paris. People point to a striking costume and say, " That is a Blum." (*Suits the action to the word and points out to the audience*).
MATHILDE :	Dear Blum—she's the only friend I have in Paris (*Looking out to audience*). What did she (*looking back at* CHARTERIS) say when you told her of our marriage ?
CHARTERIS :	Ha, ha! What did she say ! There was a scene. And what a scene! (*He rises from seat*) " Ma petite married ! To you married ! Alone in England ! Oh ! " (*He to R.C. imitates* BLUM, *stamps his feet*) " Mon Dieu—it cannot be—it cannot be. No, no, no ! "
MATHILDE :	Ha, ha ! That's just like her. (*Rises from seat and moves down L.*) Dear Blum ! Oh ! I do wish she were here now.

CHARTERIS : But, darling, haven't I told you ? She *is* here.
MATHILDE : Here ! She came *with* you ! To see me married ! Oh, how exciting ! (*Moves to L.C.*)
CHARTERIS : (*To her*) Old Tony's looking after her. He's been making furious love to her all the way here.
MATHILDE : Tony ? Who is Tony ?
CHARTERIS : Tony Chute, of the American Embassy in Paris. (*Lots of French off from* BLUM). The best fellow in the world—and my best man. I'm sure you'll like him.
BLUM : (*U./R. off*) Vare is ma Princesse ? (*On entrance*) Où est elle, ma petite princesse ? Il y a tellement longtemps que je ne l'ais vue . . . ah ! la voila—ma petite—ma 'Tilde.

(BLUM *is a fussy, middle-aged, but well-preserved Frenchwoman. She is very agitated in manner, and runs through all sorts of emotions in rapid succession. She takes* MATHILDE'S *hands.*)

MATHILDE : Oh, dear Blum !

(CHARTERIS *moves to R. of stage behind* BLUM *and* MATHILDE.)

BLUM : (*Convulsively embracing her*) Ma p'tite. ' Tilde ! And to be married. And to a nobody. (*Looking at* CHARTERIS *R.*).
MATHILDE : (*L.*) Blum ! (*Is about to be indignant*).
BLUM : No, no. No, I'm only joking. As long as he loves you ! Zat is all that matters. I vould not have consented otherwise.
CHARTERIS : I say, do excuse me, (*Feeling very embarrassed*) I must buzz along to the church. (*He Exits U./R., picking up hat, etc. from seat en route.*)
BLUM : Oh ! I like him. He's better zan zat Prince Carlo ! (*Breaks R.*)
MATHILDE : And you have come all the way to see me married.
BLUM : But certainly. Could ma Princesse be married vizout Blum ? Non. Jamais de la vie. Vould I not go to to—Madagascar to see her happy ? (*She takes* MATHILDE *over to R.C.*). Now tell me—zey have been kind to you here in England ?
MATHILDE : Oh yes ! I've made many friends. But one in particular —a little Quaker girl. (*She looks over her shoulder to Quaker house R.*)
BLUM : Quakaire ? Vat is zat ? Quakaire ? Vat is Quakaire ? Ce droll ça. Quakaire ! Ha-ha-ha.
MATHILDE : You must see her. (*Takes* BLUM'S *hand*) And how the Maison Blum ? (*Moves to L./C. with* BLUM).

BLUM :	The Maison Blum ! Formidable un succès fou. (*To C. stage*). Ah, it is — " Madame Blum vat vill be ze next mode ? " I give zem the top line, I give them the bottom line — and if I give them nothing at all they wear nothing at all ! But I 'ave for ze marriage of ma p'tite, a Blum creation par excellence !
MATHILDE :	But I was going to be married like this. (*Holding up the end of her dress*).
BLUM :	(*Definitely*) Impossible ! A Princesse ! No, no, no ! Jamais de la vie ! It is of ze simplest. Oh. Vare is he—
MATHILDE :	Who ?
BLUM :	That American ! Ah, vat a flirt ! 'E make love to me all ze time in ze train. And I liked it ! (*Crosses L.*)
	(BLUM *works over to L.C.*, MATHILDE *is C.*).
TONY :	(*Heard off R.*) Why didn't you tell me it was such a long way ?
CHARTERIS :	Sorry, old man, but I'd no idea it *was* so far.
	(*Enter* TONY, *R.2.E. with* CHARTERIS. *He carries several dress boxes and a hat box.*)
TONY :	A pity they can't raise a taxi in this village. (*Puts down hat box ; he is about to use it as a seat*).
BLUM :	Ah !
CHARTERIS :	Ah !
TONY :	Ahhh !
	(BLUM *moves to L. of* TONY *as he goes to sit on hat box.*)
BLUM :	Ah, ze wedding costume ! It vill be ruined !
TONY :	(*Picking up the boxes*). Madame ! Have no fear ! The sacred trust I assumed at the Depot shall be guarded as my life. Bon jour ! (*Is going into Inn when* CHARTERIS *calls him*).
BLUM :	Bon jour. (*Moves up to R.C. in front of tree*).
CHARTERIS :	(*C.*) I say, Tony ! I want to present you to Mathilde. Darling, this is my great friend Tony Chute.
	(MATHILDE *R. of* TONY).
	(TONY, *having his hands full, is embarrassed about taking off his hat. He, by a backward jerk, throws it off behind and* PHOEBE *Enters from Inn in time to catch it adroitly*).
TONY :	Princess, I am honoured ! Forgive my informal appearance, but the novel experience of having my arm around an unfilled costume—(*Touches box with his foot*) must plead my excuse.
MATHILDE :	(*R.C., who can't help laughing at him*) Brian has told me a lot about you, Mr. Chute.

TONY :   (*R.C.*) He's been blabbing, has he ? I am obliged to my friend for breaking me gently to you, Princess, I should have been sorry to have come upon you as a shock on this happy occasion.

MATHILDE :   It is very kind of you to have come.

TONY :   Not at all. It's very good of you to let me come. They don't let me in everywhere, you know !

MATHILDE :   Phoebe, take those things from Mr. Chute.

                (PHOEBE *relieves* TONY *of the boxes*).

TONY :   Ah, Phoebe darling ! (*Chucks* PHOEBE *under chin*) That's the other one I promised you.

                (PHOEBE *Exits with boxes through Inn.*)

BLUM :   (*To* MATHILDE) 'E's a flirt !—that one !

TONY :   (*C.* to MATHILDE) Me no flirt—it's a habit ! (*Moves C. to* MATHILDE).

BLUM :   He's a rabbit !

TONY :   Princess ! (*Taking a little jewel-case from his pocket*) Will you favour me by accepting a little cadeau de noce ? (*She takes it and crosses R. to* CHARTERIS. *To* BLUM) C'est parfait, n'est-ce pas ?

BLUM :   Splendide.

TONY :   A little French knick-knack I picked up.

MATHILDE :   (*L.*) Oh, how lovely ! Look Brian. (*Crosses to* CHARTERIS *down R.*)

TONY :   So glad you like it. That's a real pigeon-blood ruby. (*To* BLUM) I shot the pigeon myself.

                (MATHILDE *comes to* BLUM.)

BLUM :   Bravo !

MATHILDE :   And what a quaint setting ! (*Showing it to* BLUM, *C.*)

BLUM :   Ah ! Let me see, darling. It is the very brooch I 'ave so longed for to give to you, ma petite. And ven I go to Cartier's to buy it, it has been sold—and to you ! (*Embraces* TONY *in her excitement*) Oh, oh !

                (BLUM *moves to* TONY *L.C. Both embrace.* TONY *lifts* BLUM *up and down several times.* TONY *slaps* BLUM'S *bottom.*)

BLUM :   Oh, la, la ! (*Moves down L.*).

CHARTERIS :   (*L., referring to the gift*) Awfully good of you, Tony ; but (*Looking at watch*) I say, we must go !

                (PHOEBE *enters from Inn*).

BLUM :   Ah, come then, p'tite. (*Crosses to L. of* MATHILDE.)

MATHILDE :   But I did so want the little Quaker girl to see me married.

ALL :   Quaker girl ?

MATHILDE : Yes, her name is Prudence. She lives over there (*Indicating cottage R.*) with some horrid old Quakers who shut her up. Phoebe knows all about them.
TONY : (*Crosses R.*) So there are Quakers around here, Princess.
MATHILDE : (*C.*) Oh yes ! Quite a number. But you can't mistake Prudence. If you see her do please ask her to come to the church.
(CHARTERIS *comes down to her.*)
TONY : Rather ! I'll have her there with bells on.
CHARTERIS : (*R., looking at watch*) Come on—we've only got ten minutes.
BLUM : Ah, ten minutes, chérie. I vill go and get readyy our dress. One thing I ask of us all ! Be not agitated. (*Goes to Inn door and comes back to L.C.*) So. Let us all keep calm ! ! ! (*Goes to Inn door*) And don't go without me !
(*All move over to L.* BLUM *walks back, and all walk backwards with her. Bus. repeated till* BLUM *Exits through Inn door.* PHOEBE *comes down L.C.*)
MATHILDE : Oh, Phoebe, I think this is quite the nicest way of getting married, isn't it, Phoebe ?
PHOEBE : Yes, miss. (*Moves in front of* TONY—*to his L.*) A runaway match !

    TONY   PHOEBE   CHAR.   MATH.
     o   o   o   o

No. 5.—QUARTET : MATHILDE, PHOEBE, CHARTERIS, TONY.
" A Runaway Match "
(*For Movements see Dance Plot*)

MATHILDE : If this was two hundred years ago,
    In days of powder and patch,
We two would have fallen in love I know,
    And struck up a runaway match !
ALL : A runaway, runaway match !
CHARTERIS : I'd call for you at the postern door
    Discreetly left on the latch,
Then Gretna Green in a coach and four.
    And ho ! for a runaway match !
ALL : A runaway, runaway match,
A runaway, runaway match for us
    Of the good old galloping kind
When a guardian arm'd with a blunderbuss
    Is following close behind !
And all in a fury and fume and fuss
    The pair he's trying to catch
        By firing his gun away
        After the runaway,
Runaway, runaway match !
(*Dance and change positions.*)

	PHOEBE	TONY	MATH.	CHAR.
	o	o	o	o

PHOEBE : Then I'd be your faithful lady's maid,
A bundle of gowns I'd snatch,
Including a hoop and a white brocade
To wear at the runaway match.

ALL : The runaway, runaway match !

TONY : I'd drive the coach over ruts and rocks,
In a wig that's known as a scratch !
I'd look very striking on the box
In the light of a runaway match !

ALL : A runaway, runaway match
A runaway, runaway match of old
When the horses tremble and pant ;
And we're always told that the coachman bold
Must marry the confidante !
One wedding'll make many more, we're told,
And all be wed in a batch
If law hadn't done away
Now with the runaway
Runaway, runaway match !

(*Dance at end of which* CHARTERIS *and* TONY *escort the* GIRLS, *where they exit L.I.E.*)

MUSIC CUE : No. 5½.

(*Enter* NATHANIEL *and* RACHEL *R.U.E.* NATHANIEL *on R. of* RACHEL.)

NATHANIEL : Sister, the lost one—our servant Jeremiah—was not at the meeting-house. (*He begins dialogue as soon as he is in sight. They walk down to below tree, L.C.*)

RACHEL : (*L.*) Doubtless he hath been wrestling with the spirit within. (*Indicating house R.*)

NATHANIEL : Jeremiah is inclined to things of lightness.

RACHEL : Yes, he joineth our niece Prudence in the paths of waywardness.

(*Scream off, R.* JEREMIAH'S *voice is heard off in the cottage R. He enters R., laughing, excited and defiant.*)

NATHANIEL : } Jeremiah !
RACHEL :

JEREMIAH : (*R.C.*) I've done it.

NATHANIEL : } Done what ?
RACHEL :

JEREMIAH : Kissed the cook ! (NATHANIEL *and* RACHEL *horrified.*) And I don't care ! I'm only Quaker on mother's side, and father will out sometimes.

NATHANIEL : Backslider ! (*Crosses* JEREMIAH *over to R.*)

JEREMIAH : Backslider, am I ? That cook's enough to make anyone slither. And if it hadn't been for Miss Prudence, I wouldn't have stood it as long as I have, and now father's top-dog, I won't stand it any longer.—See !

RACHEL : (*L.*) Brother (*Crosses to* NATHANIEL, *in front of* JEREMIAH) were it not well that I went to comfort our handmaiden ?

JEREMIAH : Ha-ha, don't you worry. I've seen to her.
(JEREMIAH *swaggers up stage with his back to audience and shows mark of the cook's arms and hands on his back as though she had embraced him with her hands covered with flour.* WILLIAM *enters from Inn L., sees this and laughs, and* JEREMIAH *comes down C.*)

NATHANIEL : Forth from our fold, thou man of wrath !

JEREMIAH : Man of froth, am I ? Here, William. (*C.*) Bring me a large gin and ginger-beer. The gin's for father, the ginger beer's for mother.
(*Exit* WILLIAM, *chuckling, into Inn.*)
Man of froth, am I ? (*Takes cigar from his pocket—lights it, and puffs defiantly, walks down stage C., swaggeringly.*)

RACHEL : (*Down R.*) He smoketh !

NATHANIEL : (*Down R.*) He doth !

JEREMIAH : I do-eth. A cigar.

NATHANIEL :
RACHEL : } Cigar !

JEREMIAH : Yes—I won it at the fair yesterday—Cabbagio claro or a china dog.

NATHANIEL :
RACHEL : } Fair ! (RACHEL *walks up stage R. with her back to audience, in disgust.*)

JEREMIAH : Yes. Fair. And I went in to see the fat lady.
(NATHANIEL *and* RACHEL, " *Oh* " !)
And I paid twopence extra to pinch her. Oh, father's fairly let loose now. (*Sits on seat C.*)

RACHEL : Brother, our maidens come. Let not their eyes witness this spectacle of depravity. (*Turning down stage to* NATHANIEL.)

NATHANIEL : Come, let us turn our backs on the lost sheep.
(*They both walk to the Quakers' House with their backs to* JEREMIAH.)

JEREMIAH : Bah ! Bah ! He thinks I'm Larry the Lamb. (*Sits bench C.*).

MUSIC CUE : No. 6.

(NATHANIEL and RACHEL *exit into house.*)

(*The* QUAKERESSES, *with* PRUDENCE, *enter R.U.E.* PRUDENCE *is last in entering and it is arranged so that the audience do not at first identify her.* QUAKERESSES *exit into house R.* PRUDENCE *is following, when* JEREMIAH *whistles and rises from seat. She turns.*)

JEREMIAH : (*C.*) Miss Prudence ! Miss Prudence ! They've let you out at last then ? (*He stands up and walks down C.*)

PRUDENCE : (*R.*) Oh, Jerry, I have been well content. (*Turns to* JEREMIAH *and walks slowly to him, C.*)

JEREMIAH : Content ! In the meeting-house ?

PRUDENCE : Yes, I have found much within this book to beguile the time. (*Hands him the book closed, he reads the title on the back.*)

JEREMIAH : " Reflections."

PRUDENCE : It is thus named outside, Jerry, for the sake—of—convenience.

JEREMIAH : (*Looking inside*) " Reflections Of A Bright Young Thing." Any pictures ? (*He gives book back to* PRUDENCE). Sorry Miss Prudence.

PRUDENCE : Aunt Rachel saw the outside title and said she hoped I would gain much profit by it. I have—

JEREMIAH : (*Coughs*) I bet you have.

PRUDENCE : Why, Jerry ! thou art smoking.

JEREMIAH : (*L.*) I art ! (*He is very uncomfortable with his cigar.*)

PRUDENCE : (*L.C.*) It smells funny.

JEREMIAH : It tastes funny—(*Lifts cigar up*)—it is funny. I'd better throw it away—it might make you ill.

PRUDENCE : No ! I like it, Jerry.

JEREMIAH : Do you ? Then you'd better finish it, Miss Prudence !

PRUDENCE : Don't stop !

JEREMIAH : No, I won't in a minute. (*Moves L., looks round stage*) Miss Prudence. (*Takes* PRUDENCE'S *hand and brings her down stage two or three steps L.*) I—I'm going to run away.

PRUDENCE : Run away—and leave me ! Oh Jerry, what shall I do without thee ?

JEREMIAH : What shall I do without *thee*, Miss Prudence ?

PRUDENCE : Where art thou going to, Jerry ?

JEREMIAH : I don't know, miss—but now father's top-dog I should like to see a bit of life.

PRUDENCE : (*Breaks R. sighing*) At times the spirit moveth me that way too, Jerry.

JEREMIAH :	Foreign parts—you know—anywhere away from this village—
PRUDENCE :	Jerry, thee'll be so repentant tomorrow. (*Moves over to R.*)
JEREMIAH :	(*Coughs breaks L.*) I'm a bit repentant now, Miss Prudence.
PRUDENCE :	(*Returns to his R.*) Why, thou art quite pale and trembling now.
JEREMIAH :	(*Under influence of the cigar*) No ? Am I ? That's mother ; she always did object to smoking. (*Moves over to L. below Inn.*)
PRUDENCE :	What's the matter, Jerry ? Aren't thee well ? (*Goes over to him L.*)
JEREMIAH :	Oh, yes, yes, Miss—I'm quite well—quite well. Only (*Looking at cigar*) I wish I'd had the china dog instead.

(*Exit L.1.E. as though dashing away to be sick.*)

No. 7.—SONG : (PRUDENCE).
" A Quaker Girl "

Oh, a quiet Quaker maid
  From my babyhood I've been,
For I never even played,
  With the children on the green ;
But I used to sew and mend,
  Whilst my aunt was sitting near,
Till a little Quaker friend
  Came and whispered in my ear :—

" Thee loves me, and me loves thee "
  Oh, he was a young mischief-maker ;
Two little sweethearts we used to be—
  He was such a dear little Quaker !

Now, I'm quite a Quaker girl
  Very modest and sedate ;
If my hair begins to curl
  I am told to brush it straight ;
And the days are very sad,
  And the world is very grey
For there's not a Quaker lad
  Who will come to me and say :—

" Thee loves me, and me loves thee "
  None to woo a maiden and take her ;
Nobody seems to care about me—
  Life is very dull for a Quaker !

But although the Quaker men
  Do not know the way to woo,
I have fancied now and then
  There are other men who do !
If I meet with one of these,
  Then it might be very nice
When we walked beneath the trees,
  If he murmured once or twice :—

"I love thee and thee loves me,"
Love's the only true marriage maker,
Somebody's wife one day I may be
But not the little wife of a Quaker!
(*Sits on tree-seat.*)
Not the little wife of a Quaker.
(*Begins to read book.*)
(*Enter* TONY CHUTE *from L.1.E., humming. He sees* PRUDENCE *sitting at tree.*)

TONY : What a nice little girl! A Quaker girl! I wonder if she is *the* Quaker Girl. (*Takes off hat.*) Good morning! (PRUDENCE *looks up to him and back again to book.*) Ahem! (*Moving to L. and back to L.C., Assuming a very sanctimonious manner.*) Sister, canst thou give me tidings of a maiden named Prudence? (*Hands joined a la Quaker.*)

PRUDENCE : (*Sedately*) Yes, friend! What seekest thou with her?

TONY : I would e'en commune. I am the bearer of tidings. Perchance, perhaps, peradventure thy name is Prudence?

PRUDENCE : Yes, friend—and thine?

TONY : *I* was christened Anthony actually, but the lads call me Tony—Tony Chute.

PRUDENCE : Verily, friend, methinks Tony were better than Anthony.

TONY : Then you will call me Tony. (*Sits on her L.*)

PRUDENCE : (*Rises—crosses R.*) Friend, thy manners savour of the world without.

TONY : (*Following*) I prithee do not go. (PRUDENCE *looks at* TONY.) I—prithee! (*He touches* PRUDENCE'S *left hand as though looking for a wedding ring*) Thee is not —married, Prudence?
(*She stops*).

PRUDENCE : My thoughts have not dwelt on the matter of marriage, friend Tony. (*Going again, R.*)

TONY : Nay, tarry, maiden, nay, tarry, hath none of the—er— brethren talked to thee—er—of love? (*Coming closer.*)

PRUDENCE : Nay, it were unseemly—as thou, who art *apparently* of our persuasion must know. And they are too good to think of love. Art thee very good?

TONY : Don't make me laugh. (*Turning to C. stage and back to* PRUDENCE.) Dost thee like only those who are very good.

PRUDENCE : (*Sighs*) I have seen none other.

TONY : (*Aside*) Where am I? Where *am* I? (*To her*) And if thee met one who was not so very good wouldst thou like him?

PRUDENCE : Perchance ! One waxeth weary of the *very* good sometimes.
TONY : Then, Prudence, I will tell thee. (*Looking around stage*) I am not so very good. Not too good to think of love when I see thee.
PRUDENCE : Oh ! (*Crosses L., in front of* TONY) Then thee must see my uncle and my aunt. They delight in reclaiming the straying ones.
TONY : Cannot I try persuade thee to try ? (*To her*) I could listen to thee, Prudence as I could listen to none other.
PRUDENCE : Then thee must not think of worldly things.
TONY : Then I'll think of you (*Does a little bob, raises hat*) thee— thou ! (*Bows to her like a Quaker.*)
PRUDENCE : Thee must read much in good books.
TONY : Then I will devour thine ! (*Takes* PRUDENCE'S *book and moves over to R.C., looking at the title.*)
PRUDENCE : (*Dropping her Quaker tone in alarm*) No, no ! You mustn't look, please.
TONY : (*Looking at cover*) Reflections !
PRUDENCE : Please—please don't open it.
TONY : Certainly not—if you don't wish it ! (*Handing it to her— she takes book.*) But thee must exhort me all the more since I may not read.
PRUDENCE : (*Walks to down stage L., struck by his courtesy.*) Friend, thee art no Quaker.
TONY : Why ?
PRUDENCE : One of our persuasion would have opened it and read it.
TONY : No, I'm no Quaker, but if thee wishes it, I'm quite willing to become one. (*He moves over to* PRUDENCE, *L.*)

Warn Elec.

PRUDENCE : But thee is a stranger to me—Tony.
TONY : Well, we're getting over that every minute, aren't we ?
PRUDENCE : And thou wouldst embrace—
TONY : Would I ? Embrace ! (*He makes movement.*)
PRUDENCE : Our faith ? (*Takes a step back.*)
TONY : There's nothing of thee I would not embrace.
PRUDENCE : But it may be that I would not like thee as a Quaker, friend Tony.
TONY : Then like me as I am, friend Prudence.
PRUDENCE : Wouldst thou have me like thee ?
TONY : Would I have thee like me ? (*Putting his arm round her waist.*)
PRUDENCE : Nay, truly, though it be pleasing enough (*Moves in front of* TONY *to R.C.*) that is not the Quaker way. (*Moves over quickly to R. of stage.*)

" *Go* " *Cue* 1

No. 8.—DUET : (PRUDENCE and TONY)
"A Bad Boy and a Good Girl"

TONY : When a bad, bad boy like me (*To her L.*)
Meets a good, good girl like you,

PRUDENCE : Well, the good little maid
Is a bit afraid
And wonders what on earth to do.
(*Moves over to R.*)

TONY : If the bad, bad boy should speak
Will the good, good girl reply ?
(TONY *goes over to* PRUDENCE'S *L.*)

PRUDENCE : Well, it rather depends
If the good girl's friends
Are anywhere at all close by.
(*Both look around to see if anyone is watching,* PRUDENCE *to R.,* TONY *to L.*)

TONY : Such a bad, bad boy !
(*Both together again, facing front.*)

PRUDENCE : Such a good, good girl !

BOTH : Oh, they do make a curious pair.

PRUDENCE : Though the good girl may
Turn her head away, (*Turns head away.*)
Still she knows that the bad boy's there.

TONY : If the bad boy walks
By her side and talks,
Will she snub him as a maiden should ?
(*Walks L. followed by* PRUDENCE.)

PRUDENCE : Well, I think thee's a lad
Who is not so very bad,
And I'm not a bit too good !
(PRUDENCE *goes up stage C. and sits on R. of seat*).

TONY : (*L.C.*) If the good, good girl sits down,
What's the bad, bad boy to do ?
(*Moves up and sits on* PRUDENCE'S *L.*)

PRUDENCE : He must sit over there,
For the good girl's chair
Was surely never meant for two.
(*Indicates L. stage.* TONY *rises, goes L.C.*)

TONY : If the bad, bad boy comes close,
Will the good, good girl be vexed ?
(TONY *sits on* PRUDENCE'S *L.*)

PRUDENCE : (*Rising and tripping down stage R.C.*)
Well, she might run away
Or—she might just stay
And see what's going to happen next.
(*she returns C. She twiddles her thumbs,* TONY *imitates.*)

Warn Elec.

TONY : What a bad, bad boy!
PRUDENCE : What a good, good girl!
BOTH : Oh, they do make a curious pair.
PRUDENCE : If the good girl's wise,
　　She will shut her eyes
　　　When the bad boy begins to stare.
(*Puts hands up to eyes.*)
TONY : May the bad boy, please,
　　Give her hand one squeeze?
　　　For he'd like to, if he only could.
(*He squeezes her hand.*)
PRUDENCE : Oh, I fear thee's a lad
　　Who is very, very bad—
　　　Now really thee must be good!
(*She takes his hands and puts them back on to his knees.*)
(*Dance. See Dance Plot. At finish of dance,* PRUDENCE *makes a demure curtsey. He blows kiss to her. She exits into house, shutting door.*)

"*Go*" *Cue 2.*

TONY : (*R. stands and calls after her*) Miss Prudence! Now I haven't given her the message!
(*Enter* CHARTERIS *R.U.E., hurriedly and excitedly to L. of* TONY.)
CHARTERIS : I say, Tony. They're ready at the church! Where is she? (*Looks off to Inn L.*)
TONY : And to think I've crawled around all these years without knowing her. Oh, fie, fie, fie! (*He is still gazing after* PRUDENCE ; *blows a kiss to Quaker door.*)
CHARTERIS : What the deuce are you raving about? (*Moves to C., looking at* TONY.)
TONY : The dearest, sweetest girl on earth, my boy.
CHARTERIS : Are you referring to Mathilde?
TONY : No—the Quaker girl. The dear little Quaker girl. (*He moves over to cottage R. kisses doorway.*)
CHARTERIS : Look here, Chute—don't be a fool. (*Breaks L.*)
TONY : Fool! (*Moving to R.C. from cottage, R.*) How you could have wasted a moment's thought on Diane and the rest in Paris, beats me. (*Moves to* CHARTERIS *R.C.*)
CHARTERIS : I? You, you mean.
TONY : Don't interrupt. I haven't felt like this before and it might evaporate. (*Looks again at cottage R.*)
CHARTERIS : Don't stand staring there, man! Have you got the ring?
TONY : Have I got the ring? (*Moves to* CHARTERIS *R.C.*) Have I known her long enough for that?

CHARTERIS :	No, my ring ! (*Enter* MADAME BLUM *from Inn ; she is in a highly emotional state, with handkerchief to eyes.*)
BLUM :	Ooh-ooh ! Ooh, ooh !
TONY :	There's a pigeon loose somewhere. (*Looking straight out at audience.*)
BLUM :	I cannot part wiz 'er.
CHARTERIS :	(*C., to* BLUM) Isn't she ready ?
BLUM :	Yes, she is ready (*Moves to C.*) but I cannot bear to part wiz 'er. (*Enter from Inn L.* MATHILDE. *She is now dressed in the Parisian wedding dress brought by* BLUM. *She is followed by* PHOEBE . MATHILDE *comes to L. of* BLUM, *smiling happily.*)
CHARTERIS :	Oh, darling—you look beautiful.
MATHILDE :	(*L.C.*) Ah, that is Blum—dear Blum ! (*Moves to* BLUM *C.—hugs her.*)
BLUM :	(*C. Turns her round to inspect the costume.*) You look beautiful, but I cannot part with you !
MATHILDE :	Mr. Chute, have you seen Prudence ?
TONY :	(*R.*) Have I seen Prudence ? I need Prudence. (*Goes over and kisses downstage portal of house.*)
BLUM :	(*Goes to* TONY *R.*) Ah, Monsieur Tony, have you forgotten this morning you did promise to " look after me ! "
TONY :	That was this morning—early ! (*Breaks U/S.*)
BLUM :	Too early, ah ? (*Moves R./C.*) (*Enter* PRUDENCE *R. from house.*)
MATHILDE :	(*L., runs to her*) Oh, I'm so glad you're here. This is Captain Charteris. (*Brings* PRUDENCE *to C. to introduce her.*) (CHARTERIS *bows and says* " *How do you do.*" TONY *is downstage over R.*) And this is my friend Madame Blum. (*Indicating* BLUM *up stage R.*) (BLUM *is fascinated—she is evidently struck with an idea, looking at* PRUDENCE'S *dress.*)
TONY :	(*D/R.*) And this is me ! (*Joins his hands together like a Quaker.*)
BLUM :	Ah ! Voila ! Wait, I have an idea.
BLUM :	I vill make zat the fashion—the hit—the rage of Paris. (*Gesticulates excitedly. Walks round to L. of* PRUDENCE.) It vill be ze sensation—a furore ! (*To* PRUDENCE) Oh, come with me to Paris.
PRUDENCE :	I ?—to Paris ?

TONY:	*(Aside)* Prudence in Paris. She'd never get through the customs.
CHARTERIS:	*(Fidgeting about L.C.)* Mathilde *(Looks at watch)* it's getting late.
MATHILDE:	*(To* PRUDENCE*)* You are coming to the church to see me married?
PRUDENCE:	Oh, what would the Friends say?
BLUM:	*(Who is divided between her excitement at the wedding and her discovery of the Quaker costume)* But ze apron! *(L. of* PRUDENCE, *walks in front to L., lifting apron.)* Oh, chic—comme ce chic—ze apron.
TONY:	Oh! ze apron! Oh chic, chic! ze apron! *(Shakes apron.)*
MATHILDE:	But think, Prudence, my wedding! *(To* PRUDENCE.)
PRUDENCE:	Very well, then, but we must go quietly. *(Crosses to gate, listening.)* S'sh!
TONY: \ CHARTERIS: ∫	Sh!
MATHILDE \ PHOEBE: ∫	Sh!
BLUM:	Sh!

(TONY *and* PRUDENCE *sit in front of tree* CHARTERIS *crosses to* MATHILDE *R. finish DL.)*

No. 9.—CONCERTED NUMBER: (MATHILDE, PRUDENCE, BLUM, PHOEBE, CHARTERIS, TONY and CHORUS)

" Tip-toe! "

PRU.　TONY　BLUM　MATH.　CHAR.　PHOEBE
　o　　　o　　　o　　　o　　　o　　　o

(For movements see Dance Plot.)

(During the Symphony TONY *and* BLUM *waltz on R.,* MATHILDE *and* CHARTERIS *on the L.* PRUDENCE *is at gate listening ;* PHOEBE *up L.)*

MATHILDE:	Tip-toe! Tip-toe!
	  Quietly to church we go;
	Speak low, speak low!
	  Don't let anyone know.

(TONY *takes* PRUDENCE'S *left arm and goes on to bench in front of tree C.,* TONY *sitting on* PRUDENCE'S *R.)*

MATHILDE: \ CHARTERIS: ∫	Tip-toe! Tip-toe!
	  Step as light as falling snow,
	Just so! stealthy and slow,
	  On tip, tip-toe!

(VILLAGERS *enter L.U.E. in twos and threes, being enjoined to secrecy by* PHOEBE.)

MATHILDE :	We're in breathless expectation— Ready for our celebration That is now to crown our daring plans, Our daring plans. But I'm all in trepidation Lest some prying male relation Should, as you would say, forbid the banns ! (PHOEBE *drops behind to L. of* CHARTERIS.)

PRINCIPALS
AND
CHORUS :
	Tip-toe ! Tip-toe !
	  Quietly to church we go,
	Speak low, speak low,
	  Don't let anyone know.
	Tip-toe ! Tip-toe !
	  Like a noiseless shadow-show,
	Just so—silently—go,
	  On tip-tip-toe !
	(Mrs. LUKYN *and* WILLIAM *enter from Inn L. and stand in front of Inn, watching.*)

PRUDENCE :	Though they laugh
	  Light and merrily,
	I am half
	  Frightened verily !
	And in fact
	  Faint with alarm.

TONY :	Let me offer my arm !

PRUDENCE :	Our sedate
	  Friends Society
	Reprobate
	  As impiety
	Such an act—
	  So if they see—

TONY :	Then refer them to me.

PRINCIPALS
AND
CHORUS :
	Tip-toe ! Tip-toe !
	  Quietly to church we go,
	Speak low, speak low,
	  Don't let anyone know.
	Tip-toe ! Tip-toe !
	  Tripping two and two in row
	Just so warily go
	On tip, tip-toe !
	To church now we go.
	(*General exeunt on concluding symphony R.2.E. The* CHORUS *lead followed by* CHARTERIS *and* MATHILDE, *arm-in-arm* ; BLUM *and* PHOEBE ; *and lastly,* TONY *and* PRUDENCE, *arm-in-arm.*)

TONY :	(*To* PRUDENCE *as they go off*) I don't know how far this church is but I hope it's a long way. (Mrs. LUKYN *and* WILLIAM *watch the exit, then come down stage,* Mrs. LUKYN *L.C. and* WILLIAM *on her L.*)
Mrs. LUKYN :	(*C.*) Well, I must say a sweeter bride I never saw.

WILLIAM :	(*L.*) Does great credit to The Chequers, Mrs. Lukyn, mum !
Mrs. Lukyn :	Reminds me of what I was at her age, William.
WILLIAM :	Only more so, if I may say so, Mrs. Lukyn, mum !
Mrs. Lukyn :	Now, William, no compliments, you're old enough to know better.
	(*Enter* PHOEBE *R.U.E.*)
PHOEBE :	(*R.C.*) The Princess says she'd like ong plane air.
Mrs. Lukyn :	(*C.*) Oh dearie me ! Now whatever does that mean, Phoebe ? You understand French.
PHOEBE :	It means—they be going to breakfast on plain air.
	(Mrs. LUKYN *aghast*.)
WILLIAM :	I know ! It means have the breakfast out here, furrin fashion, Mrs. Lukyn, mum.
PHOEBE :	Of course, William, I said so, didn't I ?
Mrs. Lukyn :	Come along, William. (*Crosses L. and exits to Inn, followed by* WILLIAM.)
	(*Enter* JEREMIAH, *L.1.E., very rakish, singing* " *Tip-toe, Tip-toe.*")
JEREMIAH :	(*L.*) Phoebe ! (*Going to embrace her.*)
PHOEBE :	Now you be a little less free wi' your Phoebes ! I want to know what's all this about kissing the cook ?

Warn Elecs.

JEREMIAH :	It's only my free and easy way, Phoebe—you see, I'm always thinking of you.
PHOEBE :	Well ?
JEREMIAH :	And thinking of you makes me feel (*He offers to embrace her ; she retreats*). Well—it brings out father in me—it was him that kissed the cook. (*Moves over to R.C.*)
	(VILLAGE GIRLS *enter on bridge and wait there, interested. At* PHOEBE'S *exit they come down R., laughing at* JEREMIAH.)
PHOEBE :	(*R.*) Well, I want nothing more to do wi' 'ee. (*Crosses L. to Inn.*) And you can go and tell father to go and kiss his cooks and chambermaids and not dare to be so forward with a Princess's young lady—who's going travelling with her mistress on the dejunay. (*Exits into Inn L.*)
JEREMIAH :	Phoebe ! Oh, that's the sort of trouble I'm always getting into. It's this constant battle of mother and father in me : some days mother comes over and whispers into this ear " Get married, Jeremiah," and father pops round to this one, and says " Rats "

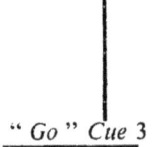

"Go" Cue 3

No. 10.—SONG : (JEREMIAH and CHORUS OF GIRLS.)

"Just as Father Used to Do."

JEREMIAH :
    I remember clearly
      Ever since a lad,
    Mother gave me good advice,
      Father gave me bad.
    Mother was a Quaker,
      Father was a rip,
    Mother kept my feet from straying,
      Father made 'em slip !
    Oh, anybody will admit
    My parents were so opposite,
      And I inherit something from the two.
    I realized, when quite a kid,
    The sort of things that Mother did
      Were not the things that Father used to do.

CHORUS :
    Oh anybody will admit
    His parents were so opposite,
      And he inherits something from the two.

JEREMIAH :
    Mamma adored her darling so
    She never smacked me hard, you know—
      Well, not so hard as Father used to do !
    Mother rose at daybreak,
      Health and wealth to win,
    Sometimes even earlier
      To carry Father in.
    Mother had a nightdress,
      Flannel, thick and red.
    Father kept a nightcap
      In a bottle by his bed.
    Oh, anybody will admit
    My parents were so opposite,
      And I'm a bit of each I must explain.
    When Mother's reason says in me
      " You've had enough," and I agree,
    It's Father's voice that bellows " Same again."

(JEREMIAH *exits L.1.E.* GIRLS *exeunt R.1.E.*)

(*Encore verses*)

JEREMIAH :
    Mother ate sedately
      All that she could take,
    Father ate enough for two
      And had a tummy ache.
    Mother had a poodle
      Walking at her heel,
    Father had an elephant
      As pink as cochineal.

CHORUS :   Oh, anybody will admit
My parents were so opposite,
  And Father in her hands was merely clay,
When Ma said Women, Wine and Song
Were bad, immoral, vile and wrong,
  Then Father gave up singing right away.

Warn Elec.

CHORUS :   Oh, anybody will admit
His parents were so opposite,
  And He's a bit of each of them, you know.

JEREMIAH :   When Mother's voice within me quotes
" It's wrong to sow your Quaker oats ",
  Then Father quickly answers " Have a go !".

(JEREMIAH *exits L.1.E.* GIRLS *exeunt over bridge.*)

" *Go* " *Cue* 4

(Mrs. LUKYN *and* WILLIAM *enter from up L., with breakfast table.*)

Mrs. LUKYN :   Now bustle up, William. They'll be back from the church directly.

(NATHANIEL *and* RACHEL *enter R.U.E. in time to see this bus.*)

WILLIAM :   Ah ! It don't take folk long to get married nowadays, Mrs. Lukyn, mum.

Mrs. LUKYN :   No, nor to get unmarried either—William—for the matter o' that !

(JEREMIAH *enters L.1.E.*)

Here you, Jerry, come and give us a hand !

(NATHANIEL *is now on* RACHEL's *L. They both walk to R.C. down stage.*)

NATHANIEL   (*R.C. to* JEREMIAH) Oh, thou reveller amid the fleshpots !

JEREMIAH :   (*C.*) Oh, thou reveller amid the chimney pots !

(Mrs. LUKYN *goes off L.U.E. and returns with two chairs which she places at table L.* WILLIAM *helps her.*)

NATHANIAL   Listen, scoffer ! Hast thou seen thy young mistress, Prudence, our niece ? (*Speaks this quicker as though agitated by the absence of* PRUDENCE.)

JEREMIAH :   (*C.*) Yea, friend Nathaniel—verily and indeed I have.

RACHEL :   (*R.C.*) Then prithee give us tidings of her.

(Mrs. LUKYN *goes off L.U.E. and returns with two more chairs and places them at table L.*)

JEREMIAH :   The spirit moveth me not to commune thereof, friend Rachel.

NATHANIEL :	(*To* RACHEL) She hath perchance lingered in the Meeting-house for further meditation, sister.
JEREMIAH :	You've said a mouthful, brother.
RACHEL :	We will thither and seek her, brother. (NATHANIEL *and* RACHEL *go up R. to house*)
JEREMIAH :	Look at them thithering !
RACHEL :	(*To* JEREMIAH) Backslider.
NATHANIEL :	Prodigal !
JEREMIAH :	Brimstone and treacle ! (RACHEL *and* NATHANIEL *exeunt R.U.E.*) Miss Prudence's meditations ain't at their Meeting-house, they're at the church and I'm going to meet her ! (Mrs. LUKYN *goes off and brings back water jug and bottle of claret which she places on table L.*) (*Enter* JARGE, *running from R.U.E., very much out of breath.*) (*Enter* PHOEBE *from Inn L.*)
JARGE :	(*To* WILLIAM) Here, William, that American gent will have a wedding peal. You're wanted for your tenor bell. (WILLIAM *moves to* JARGE'S *L. C. Stage.*)
Mrs. LUKYN :	(*By breakfast table L.*) Well, he can't come, Master Jarge—that's all. (*She goes off L.U.E. and comes back with two bottles of champagne which she puts on table L.*)
WILLIAM :	Dang it, first time I've missed tenor bell for twenty odd years. (*Moves over to L. below breakfast table.*)
JEREMIAH :	(*Goes to* JARGE'S *R.*) All right, Master Jarge—you tell me which rope to pull—and I'll make the old bell peal.
JARGE :	Come on—they be in the vestry now. (*Exits R.U.E.*) (GIRL *enters R.U.E. with lamb and stands R.*)
JEREMIAH :	Oh, there's a pretty girl ! (*Kisses* GIRL *and runs off R.U.E.*, PHOEBE, *entering from the Inn, sees this.*)
PHOEBE :	Mary Shakles, I be ashamed of thee. (GIRL *runs off above Inn R.*) Oh, she be welcome—(*Flounces over to R.C.*) I'm sure. I be that busy packing the truso.
Mrs. LUKYN :	Truso ? What's that French for ? (*To C.*)
PHOEBE :	That's French for trunk. The French lady looks at mamselle's box and says " Mong dew, what a truso." I be just going to run home to pack my tin truso. (*Runs off U/R*) (*Cheers off R.*)

No. 10¼.—BELL MUSIC for GENERAL ENTRANCE

Mrs. LUKYN : Willum ! Willum !—'ere they come.

(*Two* GIRLS *with baskets of petals and four others with handfulls of petals enter first and throw petals over* CHARTERIS *and* MATHILDE *when they enter. All the* VILLAGERS *re-enter R.U.E. and form on R. Then enter, R.U.E., to cheers,* CHARTERIS *with* MATHILDE *on his arm. During the bustle of the entrance,* TONY *and* PRUDENCE *have entered and passed to the back of the tree where they sit, unseen by audience.*)

CHARTERIS : (*Addresses all*) Thank you ! You'll all drink the health of my wife.

(*Cheers again.* CHARTERIS *embraces* MATHILDE.)

(*Enter* BLUM *R.U.E. She is supported by* JARGE.)

BLUM : (*R.C.*) Married ! Do zey marry so in England ?—Ten minutes and anyone's a wife. Ah non, Monsieur Charteris.

(JARGE *crosses behind group over to wedding breakfast table L. and exits L.U.E.*)

CHARTERIS : Madame ! (*on* MATHLIDE'S *R.*)
BLUM : That was really a wedding ? (*Doubtfully.*)
CHARTERIS : It was.
BLUM : And now vill you live 'ere, in England ?
CHARTERIS : We're going to Paris first for our honeymoon.
BLUM : To Paris ? (*Alarmed.*)
CHARTERIS : I'm on duty there.
BLUM : No, no, c'est impossible !
CHARTERIS : Impossible ! To go to Paris—why ?
BLUM : Miserable ! Do you not know ze Princess is—exiled !
CHARTERIS : Oh, the *Princess* may have been exiled, but she's Mrs. Charteris, my wife, now. (*He embraces* MATHILDE.)
BLUM : Zat matters not. Zey would turn her out of France again—ah, yes, in a few hours.
MATHILDE : Oh, Blum, what is to be done ? I won't be separated now. (*Catching hold of* CHARTERIS' *arm.*)
BLUM : Ah, zese children ! Zese children ! (*Rocking herself in her agitation.*) But yes—zere is a vay—if you are discreet. (BLUM *moves between* CHARTERIS *and* MATHILDE, *taking their hands and moves them both downstage three steps.*)
CHARTERIS : } Yes ?
MATHILDE :
BLUM : (*Mysteriously and weightily*) You will travel as one of my work girls, carrying a box, " Maison Blum." Zen if there is any question—you are one of my employees at ze Maison Blum. Voila ! C'est tout arrange ! !

CHARTERIS :	But what about me ?
BLUM :	Ah you ! You don't count. (*She turns her back on* CHARTERIS.)
CHARTERIS :	I won't be parted from my wife. (*Determinedly.*)
BLUM :	Zen zey vill part you.
CHARTERIS :	But I've taken a little cottage at Barbizon near Paris, for our honeymoon.
MATHILDE :	(*To* BLUM) Barbizon, dear Blum !
BLUM :	Vell, per'aps Barbizon—if you are discreet. And I shall 'ave ma p'tite near me in Paris after all—in spite of zem. Ha, ha ! Ze Princess Mathilde under zeir very nose. I laugh at ze Chief of Police. Ve pinch 'is nose like that—so. Ha ! very funny. (*Pinches* CHARTERIS' *nose and walks down R.*)
CHARTERIS :	Rather—great idea. (*Moves to R.C.*)
MATHILDE :	(*To* CHARTERIS) But where's the Quaker girl ? (*Moves to L..*)
CHARTERIS :	(*R.*) Yes, and where the deuce has Tony got to ? (*Turns up stage and is arrested by* PRUDENCE'S *voice.*)
PRUDENCE :	He is here, friends.
	(*They come down C.*, TONY *coming from behind tree R. and* PRUDENCE *from behind tree L.*)
	Mr. Chute was telling me of his quiet life in Paris—methinks from what he has said there must be a great number of the Friends there.
BLUM :	(*To* TONY *sarcastically*) Ha, ha ! Oui Monsieur Chute has zere plenty of friends—ha, ha ! n'est pas, Monsieur Chute ?
TONY :	Oui, oui, madame ! ! !
BLUM :	(*Moves to* PRUDENCE *L.C.*) You come zere and see for yourself.
MATHILDE :	(*L.C. to* PRUDENCE) Oh, it would be lovely if you could.
	(MATHILDE *and* PRUDENCE *move towards table, shown there by* Mrs. LUKYN.)
TONY :	I knew something was going to happen. I walked under a black cat this morning. (*Aside to* CHARTERIS) Charteris, I'm going to wipe Paris off the map. (*R. to* CHARTERIS)
CHARTERIS :	(*Aside*) So am I, after the honeymoon.
	(*Enter* PHOEBE *R.U.E. with* JIM *carrying an ordinary battered tin trunk. He crosses to L.1.E.*)
PHOEBE :	(*Up L.C.*) Put the truso in there, Jim. (*Crosses L.*)
	(JIM *takes trunk off L.1.E.*)
	(*Enter* JEREMIAH *R.U.E. with a broken church bell rope in his hand.*)

JEREMIAH :	(*Showing broken rope to* TONY).
	(MATHILDE *has come down L.C. with* CHARTERIS *during preceding dialogue and* PRUDENCE *is talking to them.*)
	I got more out of that tenor bell than ever William did. Phoebe, where are you going ? (*Coming down C.*)
PHOEBE :	I'm going to allez-toot sweet—which is French for Paris!
JEREMIAH :	(*L.*) Paris ! Miss Prudence, your uncle and aunt have been looking for you this half-hour. He, he ! They've gone to the Meeting-house. (*He goes talks to* BLUM *then goes behind tree to R.C.*)
PRUDENCE :	Oh, I suppose I'd better go. (*Regretfully comes to C.*)
TONY : MATHILDE : CHARTERIS :	No, No.
MATHILDE :	Oh, no ! You must stay to the Breakfast.
PRUDENCE :	I'm so sorry. I'm afraid I cannot. I must go back now.
MATHILDE :	Oh, I shall be so disappointed if you do, as we may not see each other for such a long time.
PRUDENCE :	All right, then ! I'll stay, but I shall have to do penance afterwards.
	(TONY *registers pleasure when* PRUDENCE *agrees to stay.*)
MATHILDE :	Mr. Chute, will you take care of Miss Prudence for me ?
TONY :	(*To* MATHILDE) With the greatest of pleasure. (*Taking* PRUDENCE'S *right arm, moves up to table L. with her.*)
	(BLUM *comes to C. from table L.C.*)
BLUM :	(*Pulling* TONY *back by the coat tails*) And vat about me ? Finish viz me ?
TONY :	(*Kisses* BLUM) Oui, madame, tres fini.
	(PRUDENCE *sits on downstage chair R. of table L.*)
	(*They all move to the table, leaving* BLUM *C.* TONY *sits L. of table on bench.*)
BLUM :	Voila ! Oubliee ! Forgotten !
JEREMIAH :	(*Comes L. of* BLUM *from behind tree R.C., looking at her doubtfully*) Nong ! Jamais ! Jamais nong ! (*Offers arm to* BLUM *and takes her over to R. of table.*)
BLUM :	Oh, Monsieur Quakaire.
	(*They go to table.* BLUM *sits on chair R.C. of breakfast table.*)
TONY :	Drinks for everyone, William, and plenty of it. We're to drink the health of the bride in good old English fashion.
	(JEREMIAH *exits above Inn.*)
	(*A* VILLAGER *returns with trayful of mugs of beer and hands the mugs round to* VILLAGERS.)

No. 11.—FINALE.

(*For movements see Dance Plot*)

(*During Symphony the* VILLAGERS *cheer as* PRINCIPALS *laugh and talk at table.*)

CHORUS OF VILLAGERS :
It's the wedding day
  Of the happy pair ;
Why they ran away
  Isn't our affair.
Wish them now they're wed,
  Happiness and wealth ;
As they've kindly said
  We may drink their health.

(CHARTERIS *hands* MATHILDE *round stage, taking her left hand as though showing her off to the* VILLAGERS. *The* GIRLS *curtsey and the* MEN *touch their caps as she passes them. When she has completed a circle she goes to* PRUDENCE *and shakes her hand—and then she walks down stage on* CHARTERIS' *L., ready for her solo.*)

MATHILDE :
(*L.C.*) It's our wedding day
  We're the happy pair ;
Feasting let us stay
  In the open air,
Where the branches old
  In the roof combine,
And the sun is gold
  In the golden wine !

CHARTERIS :
(*C.*) Come to the feast,
  Be merry while we may,
This hour at least
  We cast our fears away !
Fortune is fair, let us laugh at care,
At our wedding breakfast in the open air !

(MATHILDE *and* CHARTERIS *embrace and* VILLAGE GIRLS *dance round them in a circle during this chorus*).

CHORUS :
(*Coming more to C. as* CHARTERIS *returns to table.*)
Here's to your feast !
  We'll join you if we may,
One glass at least
  In honour of the day !

(PHOEBE *enters from Inn L. and stands by arch down L. All* PRINCIPALS *now at table.*)

Oh, this is rare
And we can do our share
At a wedding breakfast in the open air.

(MATHILDE *goes to her place at breakfast table upstage L. and sits.* CHARTERIS *follows and stands on chair R. upstage of table ready for his solo.*)

(Mrs. LUKYN *bustles about supervising everything.* WILLIAM *enters from Inn with large jugs and mugs, and serves the* CHORUS *then takes jugs off L.1.E.*)

CHARTERIS : (*On chair*)
Here's a toast to my dearest wife,
    For she is of high degree,
But she has given her heart and life,
    For love alone, to me,
A health to the bride !

ALL : (*Raising mugs and rising*) A health to the bride.
(*They drink.* CHARTERIS *sits on his chair.*)

TONY : (*Offering glass to* PRUDENCE *and quoting Omar Khayyam*) " Beneath the Bough, A Flask of Wine, A Book of Verse—and thou." (*Indicating tree under which they were sitting.*)

PRUDENCE : Nay, friend—it were forbidden—" to look upon the wine."

TONY : Would they forbid thee all the joys of life ?

PRUDENCE : (*Sighs*) It seemeth so—there can be little wickedness in just one taste—

TONY : Would I ask you if there were ? (*Again trying to persuade her to drink some wine.*)

PRUDENCE : Truly, I think not, friend Tony, but—(*Pours water from a jug into a glass, rises*)
(*Sings*) I'm a Quaker's daughter,
    So I drink the toast in water.

TONY : Oh !
(*Everyone registers alarm at the unlucky thing she is trying to do.*)

CHORUS :   In water !
She drinks the toast in water !
(TONY *snatches glass from* PRUDENCE *before she drinks, and pretends to faint.* WILLIAM *fans him with napkin.* PRUDENCE *sits again in her chair.* CHORUS *laugh, as* MATHILDE *rises at table.* PHOEBE *and* WILLIAM *also re-enter and stand by Inn door.*)

MATHLIDE : Here's health to my husband now
    The lover who won my heart,
For I am his by the wedding vow
    And none can make us part.
A health to the bridegroom !

ALL : A health to the bridegroom !
(*They stand and drink a little more.* JEREMIAH *enters L.U.E. to* PRUDENCE *with a champagne-glass and a bottle of champagne.*)

JEREMIAH :	Now do, Miss Prue, It's nice, I've tried it. You try, it's dry, With ice inside it. I know you'll like it rather, I do—and so does Father ! (*He offers bottle to* PRUDENCE *who gently declines it.*) (*Exits into Inn*—TONY *takes bottle—gives jug.*)
CHORUS :	We know you'll like it rather, He does, and so does father !
PRUDENCE :	(*To* TONY) Thy wine on me is wasted, Such things I've never tasted.
CHORUS :	Fill up and clink your glasses, We're not like Quaker lasses, Though she will not have her share, We'll gaily toast the happy pair ! (*As* JEREMIAH *is going off to Inn,* TONY *takes champagne bottle from him and gives him water jug.*)
CHARTERIS :	(*Stands and moves down stage L.*) Now one toast more—let's drink to Love ! (*Mugs raised.* CHARTERIS *goes back to his seat at table.*) (TONY *now offers* PRUDENCE *a glass of champagne.*)
CHORUS :	Let's drink to Love, to Love, to Love ! (*They now drink and empty mugs.*)
TONY :	Oh, do, friend Prue, A glass won't hurt you ! Thee knows it goes Quite well with virtue. Just one, there's nothing in it. (*Offers glass.*)
CHORUS :	Just one ! you must begin it. She will drink it, we'll be bound, To Love ! that makes the world go round.
PRUDENCE :	(*To* TONY *as she rises and takes glass*) Thee asks me so I'll agree. (TONY *rises and goes downstage L.C. on her L.*) Tho' thee is a sad mischief-maker. Talking of wine and of love to me— That is not the way of a Quaker. (*Raises glass*) To Love ! To Love ! To Love !) (*She sips on each " To Love ! " in front of table.*) Love, though I never have met you (*Down C.*) Love, that I never may meet, Those who have known You and knelt at your throne Say you are cruel and sweet

Some would be glad to forget you,
You are so sad to recall,
Ah ! be what you may,
I shall know you one day,
Love, you will come to us all !

(*During next Refrain* PRUDENCE *walks round* VILLAGERS *raising her glass to them and finishing L.C. with* TONY, *who refills her glass.*)

CHORUS : Love, you're the brightest of bubbles,
Out of the gold of the wine.
Love, you're the gleam
Of a wonderful dream
Foolish and sweet and divine !
Yet, though, the most of our troubles
Come when we answer your call
Oh all of us bow,
And we drink to you now,
Love, you are lord of us all !
Love you are lord, Love you are lord of us all !

(*Enter* NATHANIEL *and* RACHEL *and* FULL CHORUS *of* QUAKERS *from down R. and Quaker cottage.*)

(*The positions now are :*—THE VILLAGERS *are on the R.,* QUAKERS MEN *and* GIRLS *separated in C., with* RACHEL *and* NATHANIEL *L.C. Those on the terrace as before, with* JEREMIAH *added, who enters and gets R. of* BLUM.)

(QUAKERS *form up in two lines.* GIRLS *in front* MEN *behind up and down stage R. ;* NATHANIEL *and* RACHEL *in front,* RACHEL *on R. of* NATHANIEL. PRUDENCE *takes glass from her lips—and quickly gives it to* TONY. *Then crosses to R.C.*)

NATHANIEL :
RACHEL : } What is thee doing here ? (*To* PRUDENCE)
QUAKERS : Come with us this very minute !

PRUDENCE : Why are you so severe ? (*C.*)
There is nothing sinful in it.

NATHANIEL :
RACHEL : } Come away reckless maid !
QUAKERS : Do not sit among the scoffers.

JEREMIAH : (*Coming to* PRUDENCE'S *L.*)
You need not be afraid (*Points to* TONY)
Take your chance of joy that offers !
(*He gets to and remains at L. corner.*)

NATHANIEL :
RACHEL : } Leave them all upon the spot,
QUAKERS : Or we say we know thee not !

41

(TONY, CHARTERIS *and* MATHILDE *talk to* BLUM *who has been standing L.C., trying to get her to intervene with the Quakers on* PRUDENCE'S *behalf. She hands* PRUDENCE *over to L.C. and starts singing C. to Quakers.*)

BLUM : Sapristi, let zem be !
Come viz me, a Paree !

MATHILDE : Come with me ! Come to Paree ! Ah, Paree !
That is the place to see,
For love and song and life and light,
And laughter all the day and night.
Ah, Paree !
Merry and gay and free !
The flower of earth, the mother of mirth !
Paree ! Paree ! Paree !

(*All* QUAKERS, *horrified, turn backs.*)

MATHILDE: ⎫
BLUM : ⎭
Ah, Paree !
That is the place to see—*etc.*

(JEREMIAH *joins* BLUM *L.C. and they dance together during repeat of " Ah, Paree."* JEREMIAH *sits on bench in front of tree L.C. All* VILLAGERS *dance a country dance at the same time. At end all resume their group, and remain very still during the Quakers' music.* CHARTERIS *and* MATHILDE *embrace L.C. and spin around to time of music of " Ah, Paree."* PHOEBE *and* Mrs. LUKYN *dance a country dance below table L.C.* PRUDENCE *watches the dancing standing down stage L.C.*)

(*At the end of the ensemble, the* QUAKERS *turn front and come down C, as before. The other* PRINCIPALS *retire L. and the* VILLAGERS *R.* PRUDENCE *crosses and appeals to* RACHEL, *kneeling down in front of her until* CUE *" You bid me go."* RACHEL *turns her back upon her.*)

QUAKERS : Thee has chosen, it's the end ;
Thee is now no more a Friend.
Go with those that laugh and play,
Till they lead thy feet astray !
Thee may laugh and jest and scoff
That today we cast thee off,
Thee will see the end and know,
Finding no repentance. Go !

ENSEMBLE

(MATHILDE *moves from* L. *to* L.C. *as though to comfort* PRUDENCE.)

MATHILDE :
    Come, my dear,
    It isn't worth a tear,
    For if the old life's done,
    The new is begun.
    So forget ;
    You will be happy yet,
      There is another world for you to know
    Say good-bye and let them go.

QUAKERS :
    Thee has chosen, it's the end ;
    Thee is now no more a Friend.
      Go with those that laugh and play,
    Till they lead thy feet astray !
    Thee may laugh and jest and scoff
    That today we cast thee off,
      Thee will see the end and know,
    Finding no repentance. Go !

VILLAGERS AND OTHERS :
    They have said it it's the end,
    You are now no more a Friend,
    But we hope you'll find today
    You have kinder friends than they.
    Though you rather weep than scoff,
    When your people cast you off,
    You may find it's better so,
    Say good-bye and let them go !

(PRUDENCE *rises*.)

PRUDENCE :
    You bid me go ? You bid me go ?
    Then be it so !
    Whatever life may give,
    At least I'll live !—(*D/C*)

WARN CURTAIN.

(*General pleasure from* PRINCIPALS *and* VILLAGERS *when* PRUDENCE *sings* " *At least, I'll live.*")

    Life, with the love and the laughter
    Sorrow and joy that you give,
      You are my choice—(*To* TONY.)
    To regret or rejoice,
    Life, that I'm going to live !

(PRUDENCE *moves over to L.C.* BLUM, CHARTERIS *and* MATHILDE *talk to her and hand her over to* TONY *who is down stage L.*)

ALL : (*Except* QUAKERS *who turn their backs*)
Love with whatever comes after,
Gaily we answer your call,
So do what you will,
We will follow you still.
Love, you are lord of us all !

(CHARTERIS *takes* MATHILDE'S *right hand and leads her slowly from L.C. across stage to R.U.E.* BLUM *follows and* TONY *takes* PRUDENCE'S *right hand and leads her gently from L.C. to R.C.*)

(JEREMIAH *moves slowly from tree C. to R.C. followed by* PHOEBE.)

QUAKERS : Go, thee is lost to us all !

(PRUDENCE *makes one last appeal to* QUAKERS *with her left hand extended to them. They all have their backs half-turned to her.*)

ALL OTHERS : Love, you are lord of us all !

CURTAIN.

ACT II

(For positions see Dance Plot).

No. 12.—OPENING CHORUS AND SOLO (TOINETTE)

CHORUS OF
WORK GIRLS :
In this abode
Of Madame La Mode
Ev'ry thing's bustle and flurry and fuss ;
Early and late
Our customers wait,
Giving no end of commissions to us.
And if you'd try
To ascertain why
We are enjoying so great a success,
Well, let us add,
Society's mad
On a curious fad
In their style of dress.
In this abode, *etc.*

(NOTE : — *These lines may be omitted if desired.*)

ALL :
Fashions are swiftly flown ;
Novelties reign supreme.
Yesterday's
Is a by-gone phase
Today's is a perfect dream.
Gone are the shoulders bare.
Popular once awhile ;
Parisiennes fair
Decline to wear
A dress that's cut
On anything but
The Quaker style ;
The quaint little Quaker style.
Fashions are swiftly flown, *etc.*

(Just before end of music BLUM *Enters from C. doors to down C. The* LADY CUSTOMERS *run to* BLUM *and begin talking excitedly.)*

(Note re BLUM. *In Act I, she is speaking a foreign language, but in Act II she is supposed to be speaking her native language.)*

1st L.C. : Dear Madame Blum.
2nd L.C. : You *promised* me.
3rd L.C. I simply *must* have a Quakaire costume !
BLUM : I am mortified, mesdames—but I cannot costume the whole of Paris a la Quakaire in one week. Ah, non !

*(*BLUM *goes upstage C. as though to escape from them and down stage C. again.)*

(*The* LADY CUSTOMERS *implore her in pantomime, she appears to relent.*)

BLUM : Eh bien ! Tell me, Toinette, is it possible ?

TOINETTE : (*R., smiling amiably*) Oh, if Madame desires—

BLUM : (*To* LADY CUSTOMERS) Bon. Go then, mesdames, with Toinette. (*Indicates fitting rooms, L.*).

1st L.C. : Oh, so many thanks, madame !

2nd L.C. : Dear Madame Blum.

3rd L.C. : So very good of you.

(*All Exit L.1.E.*)

BLUM : (*Moves R. to* WORK GIRLS) You are tired, n'est-ce-pas ?

GIRLS : Oui, madame, tres fatigué

BLUM : Take then une p'tite quart d'heure — fifteen minutes only. Be punctual to return and then again to work.

(*Crosses to writing table L. as phone rings.*)

(*The* WORK GIRLS *murmur* " *Oh yes, madame !— A thousand thanks, madame !* " *as they run off R.2.E.*)

(*Phone continues ringing.* BLUM *moves to table . and puts receiver to her ear.*) Hello. Oui, Madame, The Maison Blum. Madame Blum qui parle. What ? You want a dress for tonight ? Certainly, madame. Come for your fitting tomorrow ! (*Put down receiver and moves over R.2.E. as phone rings again.*) C'est la Masion Blum—Madame Blum qui parle ! Oh, M'selle Diane ! ! (*Very sweetly*) Certainly, m'selle—certainly. Au revoir, m'selle ! ! (*Puts down receiver and calls* TOINETTE *who Enters R.2.E.*)

TOINETTE : Oui, madame ?

BLUM : Mamselle Diane, of the Opera, is coming to try on her new dress today.

TOINETTE : (*L.*) Bien, madame.

(PAGE *Enters R.2.E. and walks to L.C downstage, looking at* BLUM.)

(BLUM *sits on chair R. of table L.*).

BLUM : The charming Quakaire girl, Miss Prudence, has no returned from the races ?

TOINETTE : Not yet, madame.

PAGE : Madame—Monsieur Larose is on his way here.

BLUM : (*Rises.*) Monsieur Larose ! Bien !

(PAGE *turns smartly and marches up to double doors and stands.*)

TOINETTE :	Oh, la, la ! The Chief of Police !
BLUM :	Go then, Toinette, go and warn Mathilde not to come downstairs.
	(*Exit* TOINETTE *R.2.E., glancing back apprehensively, as Enter* LAROSE *L. He is a dapper little man, choleric, but very polite in manner. He walks with a slight limp.*)
PAGE :	(*As* LAROSE *enters*) Monsieur Larose. (*Exit through double doors.*)
LAROSE :	(*L. bowing most politely*) I trust, madame, it is convenient to receive me ? (*Walks downstage to R.C.*).
BLUM :	(*L.C., sarcastically polite*) Oh, monsieur, one is always enchanted to receive the honour of a visit from the Chief of Police.
	(LAROSE *indicates chair L. for* BLUM, *who takes no notice, and places the one from table R. for himself.*)
LAROSE :	(*Bows*) Madame ! (*Banging chair down*).
BLUM :	(*Not sitting*) Monsieur ! (*Banging her chair down*).
LAROSE :	(*Same bus.*) Madame !
BLUM :	(*Shortly*) Monsieur ! (*Sits*).
LAROSE :	(*Sits, and for a moment observes her ; she looks hard in front of her*) Madame has recently journeyed to England ? (*Taking off gloves*).
BLUM :	Monsieur may see, Madame has also returned from England.
LAROSE :	(*Rising and bowing*) And Paris rejoices.
BLUM :	Monsieur !
LAROSE :	Madame !
	(*Both rise and sit again.*)
	But Madame did not perhaps return from England alone.
BLUM :	(*Rising protestingly*) Monsieur !
LAROSE :	(*Deprecatingly. Rises. He politely motions her to sit, she does so. Both sit*) No, madame, you were accompanied by a young lady !
BLUM :	Extraordinary ! (*Very sarcastically*).
LAROSE :	I do not mean the charming Quaker Girl, but the other.
BLUM :	The other ?
LAROSE :	The other, madame ! ! ! The Princess Mathilde, exiled, forbidden to enter France.
BLUM :	(*Rises, affecting indignation*) Monsieur !
LAROSE :	Madame ! (*Same business of sitting down—they sit*). The Princess Mathilde was *married* in England—to a Captain Charteris—a King's Messenger. They were imprudent enough to come to France to spend the honeymoon at a little cottage at—Barbizon.
BLUM :	Monsieur—what is that to do with me ?

LAROSE :	Madame shall hear. After a honeymoon of three days at Barbizon, Captain Charteris is sent on one of his official journeys to Madrid. The cottage at Barbizon is closed—the Princess disappears—(*Leans forward to* BLUM) Where ? We do not know ! (*Throws himself back, smiling. Crosses right leg over left*).
BLUM :	Then we must find out. (*Repeating* LAROSE'S *leg bus.*) And that, Monsieur, is the end of the story !
LAROSE :	Not so madame. It is madame can finish it (*He taps his hat with his right hand*) I ask you, where is the Princess Mathilde ?
BLUM :	And if I say I do not know, monsieur ? (*She repeats* LAROSE'S *bus., tapping her left hand with her right.*).
LAROSE :	(*Rises*) Then the story ends, perhaps unhappily for madame. (*Shrugging his shoulders to C*) Madame, a police search at the delightful Maison Blum would be the most regrettable incident. (*Replaces his chair R. and moves to* BLUM'S *R. C. during speech.*)
BLUM :	Monsieur ! You would not—(*To* HIM.)
LAROSE :	Oh, madame, I do not threaten—I merely ask the assistance of madame. In consideration of my friendship to you, madame—I am conducting this enquiry personally —alone—at the moment.
BLUM :	Monsieur honours me. (*Mockingly curtseys*).
LAROSE :	Madame ! (*Bows.*)
BLUM :	Monsieur, I beg to be excused. (*Turns her back on* LAROSE *and walks to L. of table.*)
LAROSE :	(*Warningly*) Madame ! This is the second time you have defied the law—once before you smuggled the Princess into France, with no unpleasant result, but this time it means arrest and—
BLUM :	(*Defiantly*) Monsieur ! (*Points to door C.*)
LAROSE :	(*Very politely*) As madame pleases. It would be a disaster, but—(*Shrugs and goes up to double doors*) Au revoir, madame !
BLUM :	Adieu, monsieur ! (*Bows.*)
	(THEY *bow deeply to each other*—LAROSE *Exits, C. doors, with an exclamation of annoyance.* MADAME BLUM *goes up stage C.* PRINCESS MATHILDE *appears R.2.E. She is costumed exactly like the* WORK GIRLS.) Oh, but this is terrible !
MATHILDE :	May I come down ? (*Moves to R. C.*).
BLUM :	No, No ! Monsieur Larose ! He has come for you, darling.
MATHILDE :	Who ?
BLUM :	The Chief of Police.
MATHILDE :	Oh ! (*To* BLUM)
BLUM :	You are safe with Blum.

MATHILDE : Any news from my husband ? (*Sits on chair L. of table R.*)
BLUM : Any news of my husband ! (*Imitating* MATHILDE'S *tone*) So it goes on ! What a marriage for ma p'tite—Oh, Oh ! (*Crosses to C. gesticulating*).
MATHILDE : (*R.C., still sitting*) Blum, you're going to be cross.
BLUM : No, no ! I'm never cross. But a three days' honeymoon at Barbizon—Oh, la, la ! Three days ! What can you learn in three days ?
MATHILDE : And they went so quickly.
BLUM : And then this three days' husband is sent off to Madrid, while you must stay here hiding.
MATHILDE : (*Rises*) Never mind, Blum dear—Brian is coming back today—today ! (*Moves C. and takes* BLUM'S *hands.*)
(*Telephone bell rings.*)
BLUM : Go, go, go, quickly. (*Pushes* MATHILDE *R.*)
MATHILDE : (*Goes towards arch*) Why, it's only the telephone.
BLUM : (*Crossing to table L.*) Yes, I know. One cannot trust even the telephone in Paris ! (*Sits, putting receiver to her ear*) Allo ! Allo ! Yes, it is Madame Blum. Who ? Oh, so you have at last arrived, monsieur ? Yes, she is well, poor child.
MATHILDE : Blum—is it my husband ? (*Moves to* BLUM *L.*).
BLUM : Yes, it is your husband (*Moves to C. with phone*) of the three days' honeymoon. (*In phone*) Oui, monsieur, I repeat ! The three days' honeymoon.
MATHILDE : (*Following* BLUM) Blum, I must speak to him. Oh, do let me.
BLUM : (*In phone*) Monsieur, monsieur, she comes ! (*Walks back to table*) No answer ! (*Hangs up receiver*) V'la ! He has gone ! (*Shrugs her shoulders.*)
MATHILDE : They have cut us off ?
BLUM : Yes.
MATHILDE : And I had such a lot to say to him. (*Crosses R.*)
BLUM : Ha ! I had only just started ! (*Picks up letter from table L. and reads it.*)
MATHILDE : Phoebe !
(*Runs excitedly to* PHOEBE *as she Enters at L.2.E. humming. She carries a posy of flowers.*)
Phoebe, have you seen him ? How does he look ? When is he coming ?
PHOEBE : (*Gives posy to* MATHILDE). He sent you these, and he'll be back in Paris in a few hours.
MATHILDE : (*As she Exits R.*2.E.) Let me know the moment he arrives, Phoebe, as I mustn't keep him waiting.

BLUM :	(*To C.*) Tell me, Phoebe, did anyone follow you ? (*Secretively*).
PHOEBE :	Follow me ? I should think they did, madame. That's what I like about Paris. It's a girl's own fault if she's lonely here. (*Moves from C. to down R.C.*)
BLUM :	Take care, Phoebe, the Chief of Police looks for the Princess, your mistress.
PHOEBE :	Why, whatever for ?
BLUM :	(*R.*) They would send her out of France again. The Chief of Police, Larose, has been *here*. Aha ! He is clever but I am also no fool. (*Moves to below table L.*)
PHOEBE :	If he comes here how shall I know him ?
BLUM :	The Chief of Police walks so. (*Imitating* LAROSE'S *limp, crosses L.*)
PHOEBE :	(*R.*) Limps ?
BLUM :	(*Nodding*) With one leg, so ! Phoebe (*To behind Table*) take care, beware, look out for the man who limps— with one leg—so ! (*Exits, limping, L.1.E., hopping on right foot, one hop on each of her last three words.*)
PHOEBE :	(*Crosses L. and down below table*) Limps with one leg, does he ? I'll make him limp with two ! (*Enter* JEREMIAH *at double doors L. and down R. He has a box of chocolates tied with ribbon and a very fancy lady's garter in his pocket. Walks swaggeringly round R. C. stage.*)
JEREMIAH :	(*Tapping stick on floor, not seeing* PHOEBE) Shop ! Shop !
PHOEBE :	(*Moving to L.C.*) Jeremiah !
JEREMIAH :	(*R.*) Aha, Phoebe—how do you like my get-up ? I say— aren't the people clever over here ? Even the kids speak French !
PHOEBE :	(*L.*) Oh, Jeremiah, what would they say in the village ?
JEREMIAH :	Nothing, it would knock them speechless ! What do you think of it for the Boulevards ? (*Breaks R.*)
PHOEBE :	What are you supposed to be ?
JEREMIAH :	Well, I'm not quite sure yet. Madame Blum says I am to walk about with impressmong. I don't know who she is yet.
PHOEBE :	If I catch you walking about with anyone like that, you look out.
JEREMIAH :	You see, Miss Prudence and I are so much run after in Paris—we only mix with the real Bong Tongers.
PHOEBE :	(*To C.*) You be careful, Jerry—and keep your eyes open for a man who limps. (*Imitates* BLUM).
JEREMIAH :	Limps ? (*Sits.*)

PHOEBE :	Yes, he's a policeman—or something like that—who wants to arrest the Princess and turn her out of France, and me as well, I suppose.
JEREMIAH :	Don't you worry about that—you're both quite safe—I'm always about.
PHOEBE :	Oh ? You're always about, are you ? Well, where were you last night ? (*Crosses behind* JEREMIAH *over to R. behind table R., resting her chin in her left hand, leaning on the table,* JEREMIAH *sits on chair L. of table R.*)
JEREMIAH :	(*Smothering a laugh*) Well, you see, Phoebe—(*He looks to his left and thinks* PHOEBE *has gone. He calls* " Phoebe ! " *No answer.*) Oh ! she's gone ! Oh what a night last night ! (*He turns round R. and does* " a take ") Oh Phoebe ! ! I was looking for father !
PHOEBE:	Looking for father ?
JEREMIAH :	Yes, the last I heard of him was that he was working in Paris.
PHOEBE :	Work ? Did your father work ? (*Incredulously.*)
JEREMIAH :	Yes, he was a stockbroker.
PHOEBE :	What is a stockbroker ?
JEREMIAH :	He's a man that buys something he can't get—with money that he hasn't got—then he sells what he never had—for more than it ever cost—it's all governed by what they call the boom and the slump.
PHOEBE :	What's that ?
JEREMIAH :	Well, a boom means oysters, champagne and a bird, and a slump means winkles, Wincarnis, and the wife. (*Moves C.*) The boom's still on. I've brought you a present.
PHOEBE :	Oh, did you, Jerry ? That was kind of you.
JEREMIAH :	A box of chocolates. There ! (*Giving her the box of chocolates and at the same time unconsciously dropping the garter, turns his back on* PHOEBE *and handles things on table L.*)
PHOEBE :	Oh, I love chocolates. (*Sees garter, picks it up, looks for the other*) It's very pretty, but there's only one, and one's no good to me, Jerry. (*He is turned away*).
JEREMIAH :	You don't expect a dozen boxes of chocolates, do you ?
PHOEBE :	I don't mean the chocolates, Jerry—but the—(*very simperingly*)—the other.
JEREMIAH :	What other ?
PHOEBE :	Oh, you know.
JEREMIAH :	I'm blest if I do !
PHOEBE :	I don't like to tell you, Jerry—did you drop the other ?
JEREMIAH :	(*Exasperated*) The other what ? (*Turns to* PHOEBE).

PHOEBE : The other—(*Her back is turned to him. Hands him garter very slowly—without looking at him*)—this ?
JEREMIAH : (*Confused*) Well, you see, not knowing your exact size, Phoebe, and not having a chance of finding out your exact size, (*Puts right hand on Phoebe's left leg—she giggles*) I brought one on approval.
PHOEBE : What !
JEREMIAH : I made an appointment last night—I mean I told the girl in the shop I'd take one on approval—and I'd come back for the other.
PHOEBE : Well, you give me the address of that shop—and I'll go myself. (*Takes garter, feels it.*) Why, it's still warm !
JEREMIAH : Well, it was a hot bit of shopping ! Well, you see, Phoebe, I went into so many and I had to buy a lot of things, because I couldn't remember the French word for "no."
PHOEBE : Well, couldn't you shake your head in French ?
JEREMIAH : I tried that once and I got my face slapped twice. But I've just rememberff the name of the shop—I'll go by the back way and get you the other. Bargain Basement. Ladies' Lingerie. Going Down ! (*Exit C. doors.*)
PHOEBE : I suppose his father's wearing the other one ! (*Moves down L. and puts garter on table, L.*)

No. 13.—SONG : (PHOEBE and CHORUS OF WORK GIRLS)
" Or Thereabout "
(*For Dance—see Dance Plot*).

  Paris is the best of Cities,
   Ev'ry shop
   Is tip top !
  You can buy such pretty-pretties,
   Or a hat
   Big as that !
  You can study Paris life
  But you'd better go without your wife.

(*Enter the* SIX WORK GIRLS—THREE *R.1.E.,* THREE *L.1.E. They form as a back ground for* PHOEBE *and dance a movement.*)

PHOEBE : As you walk along the Champs Elysees or the Avenue de l'opera,
  Or thereabout,
GIRLS :   Or thereabout.
PHOEBE : You can buy French papers too with pictures of the sort of girls
  I don't exactly care about.
GIRLS :   Don't care about.
PHOEBE : What they say about them is in French of course,
  That I cannot make out.
  But I guess just what it means—

ALL :	Or thereabout !
PHOEBE :	If you pine for something smarter In the ways Of Cafés, You can go about Montmartre, There's a heap Pretty steep ! I can give the latest news. Of the pieces that they call Revues. You go round the Cafe de L'Abbaye, the Chat Noir, or the Cafe de Rat Mort, Or thereabout.
GIRLS :	Or thereabout.
PHOEBE :	All the English who are so respectable at home are pretty sure To be somewhere about.
GIRLS :	Somewhere about.
PHOEBE :	You should see them roll about with laughter as They clap their hands and shout, When dancers go like that (*kick*)
ALL :	Or thereabout !

(DANCE *and Exit R.1.E.*)

(PAGES *open doors. Enter* DIANE, *at double doors. She is in a furious temper—Crosses R.* TONY *follows— chucks* PAGE *under chin. They are both arguing as they enter.*)

DIANE :	(*R.*) Well now, I saw you.
TONY :	(*L.C.*) You saw me, what of it ?
DIANE :	You don't know her.
TONY :	No, but it's my brother's hat, and he knows her.
DIANE :	(*R., raging*) Did you see them round this Quaker Girl at the races ?
TONY :	I did ! But I couldn't get near her myself.
DIANE :	All of them—Prince Carlo, who fought two duels on my account—Monsieur Duhamel, the Minister—all those who swore devotion to me—round her !
TONY :	Not all, Diane—not all ! Have I been able to leave your side for a moment.
DIANE :	(*Moves up to* TONY's *R., and pushes him down stage R. a step on each " No "*) You ! Do you think I cannot see that this Quaker Girl has caught you too ? But she shall not have you ! The others—yes, but you— no, no, no. (*Stamps foot and goes R.*)
TONY :	(*Aside*) The no's have it. (*Aloud*) Say, Diane, I saw the nicest necklace in the world in the Rue de la Paix— shall we—?

DIANE :	(*R.*) Ah, do I want your presents, your necklace? It is revenge I want — revenge. (*Crosses to him*) Do you hear? Revenge? (*Moves down to R.C.*)
TONY :	I heard you the first time.
DIANE :	Oh, this Quaker Girl—I could—And you who swore.
TONY :	I'll swear again if you're not very careful.
DIANE :	(*Crosses to* TONY. *Puts right arm around his shoulder, strokes his chin*) My Tony, you want to please me—to make me happy?
TONY :	(*R.*) Oh, be careful. Somebody might come in.
DIANE :	You wish to make me a present, hein?
TONY :	My dear girl, any number of presents. Let's get away from here and buy them. (*He bustles her U/S.*)
DIANE :	Oh no! It is much more simple. I want you to buy me a gown that Madame Blum is making for me!
TONY :	A gown?
DIANE :	Will you come and see me try it on? (*Moves to R.1.E. and Exits.*)
TONY :	Certainly, my dear, I'll try it on you myself. (*Exits R.1.E. following* DIANE.)

(THE PAGES *Enter, one from L.2.E., one from R.2.E. and open double doors C. They remain for Number.*)

No. 14.—GENERAL ENTRANCE AND CHORUS.
"On Revient de Chantilly"

WORK GIRLS :	On revient de Chantilly! Coming from the races. They have won, as we can see By their happy faces! On revient de Chantilly! All of them are winners; There'll be gloves for us, may be, Gowns and little dinners! On revient de Chantilly! Coming from the races. They have won as we can see By their happy faces (NOTE :— *These lines may be omitted if desired.*)
MEN :	We're back from the races With pockets and cases All bursting with money we're dying to "blew." And, girls, we assure you We'll always adore you If you will allow us to spend it on you.
ALL :	And it's all through the luck of our Mascot and maiden Our hearts are so light and our purses so laden, The layer, the backer, the wily bookmaker, They're left at the post by the dear little Quaker!

	(We) (They) followed the luck of our cute little Quaker

(We)/(They) followed the luck of our cute little Quaker
And won all the money of every bookmaker.
So let's celebrate our Parisienne Ascot
    By buying (you)/(us) all souvenirs of our Mascot !
(Enter Parade of Quaker Dresses C.)
Here's the very latest fashion
Every man is sure to love ;
Modesty concealing passion
In the plumage of the dove.

GUESTS
MALE AND
FEMALE :
    And if we may add a word, a
      Girl is never too demure.
    You can get away with murder
      If you look extremely pure.

ALL : Now that Paris approves of the Quaker-Girl manner,
The Continent's certain to follow her banner ;
So Queen of the Fashions we readily make her,
    And all of (us)/(you) dress like a sweet little Quaker
Petite little, neat little Quaker.

(The MANNEQUINS join other LADIES as enter at double doors PRINCE CARLO with PRUDENCE, followed by MONSIEUR DUHAMEL. PRINCE CARLO is a distinguished but dissipated-looking man of about thirty. DUHAMEL is a white-haired characteristic " Senator.")

    DUHAMEL.   PRUDENCE.   PRINCE.

PRUDENCE : (*R.C., to* PRINCE) I must thank you, Prince, I have enjoyed it all so much.

DUHAMEL : (*R.C.*) Ah, mamselle, you have Paris at your feet—(*Sets chair at table*)

PRUDENCE : (*With a return to her Quaker manner*). Thou art very kind, friend. (*Sits*).

(DUHAMEL *goes up R.C. and talks to some* MEN *and* GIRLS *who come to him.*)

(*To* PRINCE) I am so glad that beautiful horse of thine won.

PRINCE : (*C.*) Ah, mamselle, when it is a question of beauty—I have a reputation for selection. (*Breaks L.*)

(*Enter* MADAME BLUM *L.1.E. She is received by* EVERYONE *with acclamations.* PRINCE *goes to* LADIES *L. and chats with them and puts his hat, stick and gloves on table L.*)

BLUM : Oh, la, la. (*L.*) Voila ! Did I not prophesy ? (*Walks to* PRUDENCE, *C.*)

PRUDENCE : Oh, dear Madame Blum, I have enjoyed myself so much, everything and everybody is delightful here. Paris is lovely.

BLUM : Ah bien ! But—take care of the Prince.

PRUDENCE :	He has been taking care of me all the afternoon. I've won ever so many bets. Oh, what would Aunt Rachel say ? (*Aside*) Where is the Princess ?
BLUM :	S'sh ! Not a word of the Princess here. It was to him—the Prince—they would have married her.
PRUDENCE :	Oh, and now he talks as though he wanted to marry me.
BLUM :	To marry you. No, no, that is not his way.
A GUEST :	Oh, Madame Blum.
BLUM :	But—I must now talk to my customers. (*Moves up and over to group R. and talks to different* LADY CUSTOMERS *as the* PRINCE *and* PRUDENCE *converse*).
PRINCE :	(*Moves from group L.C., down to* PRUDENCE *C.*) This, then, is your first visit to Paris, mamselle ?
PRUDENCE :	(*R.*) Oh yes ! This is the first time I've been away from my village in England.
PRINCE :	It must now be desolate. You will allow me, I hope, to do what I can to make your stay here a pleasant one ?
PRUDENCE :	You are very kind, monsieur, but I must not let your kindness make me forget that I am, after all, only a Mannequin of Maison Blum.
PRINCE :	That, dear Miss Prudence, is easily altered.
PRUDENCE :	I don't understand, monsieur.
PRINCE :	Give me an opportunity of explaining later, I beg. (*Crossing to* PRUDENCE *R.*) Meanwhile, mamselle, I wish to ask you something. Will you honour me by coming to my dance tonight ? It will be the happiest moment of my life.
PRUDENCE :	A dance ! Oh, but I've never been to a dance, monsieur.
PRINCE :	(*C.*) Then give me the pleasure of enjoying your first impressions.
PRUDENCE :	(*R.*) I should like to go to a dance.
PRINCE :	It is arranged then. (*To the Company*) Mesdames et Messieurs ! ! I give a dance this evening at the Pre Catalan, will you all give me the pleasure of your company ? (*Moves over to Group L.C. There is a general murmur of thanks.*)
DUHAMEL :	(*L., coming to* PRUDENCE) Mamselle, let me give you a little advice. Take care of the Prince. These little suppers and dances are called " His Highness's mousetraps."
PRUDENCE :	" Mousetraps " ! Thank you, monsieur, I promise if I go to this dance I'll be very careful.
DUHAMEL :	And if I can be of any service to you, please remember it will be a pleasure. (*Kisses* PRUDENCE'S *hand*) Adieu, mamselle !

PRUDENCE : Adieu, monsieur.
(DUHAMEL *Exits R.1.E.*).
PRINCE : (*Moves to* PRUDENCE, *C.*) Mamselle, let me give you a little advice—Monsieur Duhamel is—still—dangerous !
PRUDENCE : (*With her Quaker manner*) That is most kind of thee both.
PRINCE : Both ?
(MADAME BLUM *sees the* PRINCE *in conversation with* PRUDENCE.)
PRUDENCE : (*Rises to C.*) He said thy dances were called " mousetraps" and I—er—then he said, " adieu." (*Exits R.1.E.*)
BLUM : (*Dropping down*) Excusez moi, monsieur—nous sommes tres " bizzy " aujourd'hui—nous avons beaucoup a faire, nous sommes tres occupées !
PRINCE : I hope, madame, you will allow your young ladies to come to my dance tonight ?
BLUM : With pleasure, monsieur, but what about me ?
PRINCE : Oh, madame, your invitation is understood.
BLUM : Then I shall come on one condition.
PRINCE : What is that, madame ?
BLUM : That you will dance with me all the evening. (*Moves over to R.*).
PRINCE : Ha, ha ! Why am I so honoured ?
BLUM : Something tells me you need all the honour you can get ! (*Exit R.1.E.*)
PRINCE : Then, mesdemoiselles, this evening at the Ball.

No. 16.—SONG : (PRINCE and CHORUS).
" Come to the Ball "
(*For movements see Dance Plot*).

Come with me, come to the ball,
Music and merriment call.
Golden and gay are the lamps above,
Every tune is a song of love !
Ladies that come to the ball,
I am in love with you all.
Each has a part of my heart
At the ball, at the ball !

Come to the dances,
Come while you may,
Flow'rs and romances
Fade with the day ;
Come in your beauty,
Fair as a rose,
Dancing's a duty
Ev'ryone owes !
Leave me not lonely
When I implore.

	You are the only Girls I adore ! I will be loyal, True to you all, Hailing you royal Queens of the ball.
CHORUS :	Hailing us Queens of the ball.
PRINCE :	Say, will you came to the ball ? Who will not answer the call ? Join in the maze of the waltz that whirls, Gallant young lovers and laughing girls. All of you come to the ball, There will be welcome for all Chance for a dance and romance At the ball, at the ball !
CHORUS :	Yes, we will come to the ball, None but will answer the call, All of us long for the waltz that whirls, Gallant young lovers and laughing girls. Ah, let us come to the ball, There will be joy for us all, Chance for a dance and romance, At the ball—at the ball.

(*At the beginning of the last refrain* THE PAGE *on L. of double doors goes down to table L. and picks up the* PRINCE'S *hat, stick and gloves and returns to double doors and gives the other* PAGE *the* PRINCE'S *hat.*) REFRAIN *repeated for Dance.*

(THE GUESTS *walk off in pairs all exits—except double doors C.*

THE MANNEQUINS EXIT—THREE *R.*1.*E.*

THREE L.1.E.

THE PAGES *walks down stage, one R.C., one L.C.*

THE PAGE *on R.C. hands* PRINCE *his hat.*

THE PAGE *on L.C. hands* PRINCE *his stick and gloves.*

Then they both walk back smartly to C. doors and open them for PRINCE *to exit at end of Number.*

When the PRINCE *Exits—they go out closing the doors behind them.*)

(CHARTERIS *Enters L.*1.*E.* PHOEBE *enters R.*2.)

CHARTERIS :	Phoebe ! Where's your mistress ?
	(*Before* PHOEBE *can answer,* TONY *Enters R.*2.*E.*)
TONY :	Phoebe, where's Miss Prudence ? I must see her. (*Sees* CHARTERIS).
	(PHOEBE *comes down to R.*)
CHARTERIS :	(*C.*) Chute, where is she ?
TONY :	(*L.*) At Rumpelmayer's.

CHARTERIS : My wife at Rumpelmayer's ?
TONY : Your wife, man, no ! Diane !
CHARTERIS : Diane ! Oh, is that still on ?
TONY : Of course it's still on. She worships the very ground—that's coming to me. (*Crosses L.*)
CHARTERIS : (*Turns to* PHOEBE) Phoebe, go and tell your mistress I am here. No, tell me where she is, and I'll go myself.
PHOEBE : Which'll I do first ?
TONY : (*Moves across in front of* CHARTERIS) Go and find Miss Prudence, Phoebe, and I'll show you five dollars.
CHARTERIS : (*Pulling* TONY *round to L. C.*) Look here, Chute—you haven't been separated from your wife after a three days' honeymoon.
TONY : No, it'll take me all my time to get separated before I can begin it !
CHARTERIS : Now, Phoebe, where is your mistress ?
PHOEBE : (*Pointing upstairs*) She's up there, sir.
CHARTERIS : Go and tell her I'm here.
(PHOEBE *Exits*).
TONY : (*Both L.D/C.*) Look here, Charteris, this isn't fair. You're married and fixed up all right—I'm in a deuce of a mess. There's Diane at Rumpelmayer's—toying with a crumpet and working herself up into a towering rage.
CHARTERIS : That's all right, old man, don't you worry.
TONY : All right, you worry for me. (*Breaks L.*)
CHARTERIS : When I've time, but today I'm taking Mathilde back to Barbizon. (*Moves to R.2.E.*)
(*Enter* BLUM *R.2.E.*)
BLUM : Monsieur, it is impossible for you to be here. You must go, go ! (*Pushing* CHARTERIS *up to doors C.*).
CHARTERIS : (*Going down L.*) But I've come for my wife. We're going back to Barbizon.
BLUM : No, no. It is impossible.
PHOEBE : (*Running on from R.2.E. to L. of* BLUM—*shouting*) Madame Blum ! I think I've seen the man with the limp !
CHARTERIS : Oh, I must see her. (*Exits R.2.E.*)
BLUM : (*Bounding after him*) No, no, monsieur, not that way. Those are the apartments of my girls. (*Exit R.2.E. followed by* PHOEBE *shouting* : " Madame Blum ! Madame Blum ! "*)
(PRUDENCE *Enters R.1.E., walks to R.C.*)
PRUDENCE : How do you do, Mr. Chute ?
TONY : How do you do, Miss Prudence ? (*Raises hat*).

PRUDENCE : This is the first time we've met today, (*She moves over to R.C.*) though I did see you at the races.
TONY : (*Moves to C. during this speech*) It must have been over the heads of the crowd of men all round you.
PRUDENCE : They were rather nice to me. (*Crosses L.*)
TONY : Prince Carlo, especially. Do you know he's—(*Moves R.C. to her.*)
PRUDENCE : Ha, ha ! You're going to warn me against him—
TONY : I was.
PRUDENCE : That's just what he did about you. That's what all the men here do about each other. (*Sits L. of table R.C.*)
TONY : I know ! The he-cats ! I saw him pointing to me—and the lady I was with. (*Breaks L.*)
PRUDENCE : Who was it ? (*Looking round at* TONY).
TONY : The lady who was with me !
PRUDENCE : But why did she glare so at me ?
TONY : Because she knew I was thinking about you all the time.
PRUDENCE : Were you ?
TONY : Every moment.
PRUDENCE : I thought about thee—once or twice.
TONY : Did you ? (PRUDENCE *nods.*) You just make me the happiest man in the world when you say that. (*He walks to R/C.*)
PRUDENCE : (*Rises and crosses over to D/R.*) They say thee talks to many maidens thus, friend Tony.
TONY : There are no other maidens like thee to talk thus to— friend Prudence. (*Moves over to* PRUDENCE'S *L.*).

Warn Elecs.

PRUDENCE : Verily ?
TONY : Verily !
PRUDENCE : Oh, this is Paris, and everyone says such nice things to me.
TONY : Let's leave Paris, and I'll say them somewhere else.
PRUDENCE : Oh, but I don't want to leave Paris. I'm having such a lovely time here. I've been asked to go to a Ball tonight.
TONY : A Ball ! Promise me you won't go. Say you won't dance with anyone but me.
PRUDENCE : No, I cannot promise that. (*Smiling*).
TONY : You cannot, Prudence ?
PRUDENCE : Nay, because I do not know how to dance—even with thee.
TONY : Then I will show you. (*Puts hat and stick on table L.*)

" *Go* " *Cue* 5.

No. 17.—DUET : (PRUDENCE and TONY)
"A Dancing Lesson."
(For Movements see Dance Plot)

PRUDENCE :	(*L.*) Will you kindly tell me how I Should do ?
TONY :	(*R.*) Well, you take a step, take a step, take a step.
PRUDENCE :	I have taken one, and now I Take two !
TONY :	Take another step, take a step, take a step !
PRUDENCE :	I'm afraid you'll find me sadly Too slow !
TONY :	Only take a step, take a step, take a step !
PRUDENCE :	I am doing very badly I know.
TONY :	Oh, no !

(*They dance a la Polka as they talk.*)

PRUDENCE :	Is that right ?	
TONY :	Rather, do you like it ?	
PRUDENCE :	I could die dancing.	
TONY :	I shall if you don't keep off my feet. We're turning now.	(*Spoken*)
PRUDENCE :	Which way ?	
TONY :	Follow me ? (*They separate*).	

TONY :	(*Sings*) Now suppose that we take Up the waltz ?
PRUDENCE :	I'm afraid I shall make Many faults !
TONY :	Never mind the amount— Hold to me ! And remember to count, One, two, three !
BOTH :	I'll remember to count One, two, three. (*Spoken*) One, two, three—One two, three ! (*Sung*) Now we'll try !
PRUDENCE :	Oh, you will drop me, (*She slips*)
TONY :	Not I ! (*He catches her*)
PRUDENCE :	After a day of it I'll get the way of it
BOTH :	Bye and bye !

PRUDENCE : (*Dancing again*)
I'm really learning how it's done,
It seems to me delightful fun !
And if it does not weary you,
Once more we'll take it through.
(*First part of waltz, dancing*)
I am sure to make a blunder
Somehow.

Warn Elecs.

TONY : Only take a step, take a step, take a step !
PRUDENCE : Am I going right I wonder
Till now ?
TONY : Yes, you take a step, take a step, take a step !
PRUDENCE : You're a perfect dancing master
For skill.
TONY : Only take a step, take a step, take a step !
PRUDENCE : Now, I'd like to try it faster,
BOTH : We will !
(*Repeat of Polka, dancing.*)
(*Exeunt* PRUDENCE *and* TONY *R.1.E.*)

"*Go*" *Cue 6.*

(*Enter* JEREMIAH *at double doors.*)

JEREMIAH : (*Coming down to R.C., looking at red garter*) I've got it !
Oh ! What a night last night was. Oh, father did
enjoy himself. (*Does a little comic step*).

(*Enter* LAROSE, *at double doors. He is now dressed as a
wild Bohemian of Montmartre, a very extravagant type,
most effusive in manner.*)

LAROSE : (*L., theatrically*) Ah ! le cher Anglais. (*Advancing as
though to embrace* JEREMIAH.)
JEREMIAH : (*R.*) Eh ? Share who (LAROSE *kisses him. Fending him off.*)
Please ! Please ! I didn't know you cared.
LAROSE : You remember—last night—ha, ha, Viveur ! (*Digs him
in the ribs*) Viveur !
JEREMIAH : Yes, I know Ve-ver. (*Grimace and gesture suggesting
headache*) but—I don't remember you. (*Shaking head*).
LAROSE : Aha ! Montmartre ! Café de Nez Rouge !
JEREMIAH : (*Getting alarmed*) Don't speak so loud. What about it—
what about it ?
LAROSE : The tour of the Lake—the Caverns—you remember, eh ?
And in the taxi with little Fifi. (*Digs* JEREMIAH *in the ribs*)
Oh, ho !
JEREMIAH : Yes, she was a bit fi-fi-ish ! But how do you know ?
LAROSE : Ah ! Did I not bring you home ? Did I not find the keyhole
for you ? Did you not make me promise to come and see
you today ? Vive les femmes ! Vive l'amour ! Je
t'adore !

Jeremiah :	Shut the door !
Larose :	Lamour ! Lamour !
Jeremiah :	To-night for sure.
Larose :	Ha, ha ! We'll have another night of it tonight. (*Enter* Phoebe *R.1.E., unseen by them ; she starts on seeing* Larose.) (*Not seeing* Phoebe) And we will dance the jolly can-can once again ! (*Does so L.*) (Jeremiah *commences to do so also, but in turning R. comes face to face with* Phoebe. Larose *continues dancing and sits exhausted on chair R. of table L., cooling himself with handkerchief.*)
Jeremiah :	Phoebe ! (Phoebe *points to* Larose's *limp*, Jeremiah *fails to understand.*)
Phoebe :	(*Whispering to* Jeremiah) The man with the limp. The Chief of Police ! (Jeremiah *is suddenly sobered and now* Larose *turns R. and sees* Phoebe.)
Larose :	(*Bowing*) Mamselle—enchanté. (*Rising from chair*).
Phoebe :	(*With a very broad country manner*) Is the gentleman a friend of yours, Jerry ?
Larose :	Ha, ha ! A camarade ! Yes ! Ha, ha ! I meet monsieur last night and he tells me of a charming princess here. (*Twirling moustache*).
Phoebe :	(*Affecting vanity*) Princess ! Here (*Looks about*).
Jeremiah :	(*Same business*) Princess ! Here,
Phoebe :	The gentleman can't mean me, Jerry ? (*Walking round R. a la mannequin*).
Jeremiah :	Princess—ha, ha ! We've no Princess here, and you mustn't be caught here either. (*Bus. getting hold of* Larose's *collar and wheeling him round stage till he gets him between them.*)
Phoebe :	(*R.*) It would be as much as our place be worth. (*They bustle him up to double doors, C.*)
Jeremiah :	(*L.*) Oh, Madame Blum would sack us tout-de-suite !
Larose :	(*C.*) May I propose a little refreshment ?
Phoebe :	What do you say, Jerry ?—Get him out of here ! (*Bus : of pointing to the doors*).
Jeremiah :	Yes, that's it—you go and wait for us—(*Whirling him to L.*
Larose :	At the Café at the corner of the street ?

JEREMIAH : That's it.
LAROSE : You won't be long ?
PHOEBE : No—be sure not to go till we come.
LAROSE : Mamselle ! *(Bows)* At the Cafe at the corner of the street.
(JEREMIAH prepares to kick LAROSE as he is bending to PHOEBE. LAROSE turns and catches him as he has his foot poised for kick. Exit LAROSE at double doors. He disposes of his wig, cap and beard and gets ready to re-enter.)
JEREMIAH : *(Calling after him and closing doors)* Mind you wait for us !
PHOEBE : We shan't be more than a day or two.
(They take hands and dance a step of triumph round the stage, singing : " Vivons, vivons, Monsieur Larose ! Vive le vin, vive les femmes, vive l'amo-oo ! —last syllable as LAROSE Re-Enters at double doors C.)
LAROSE : Ah !
(PHOEBE shrieks and runs to table R. hiding beneath it. JEREMIAH does same to table L.)
So—you know me. Well, Monsieur Jeremiah and Mamselle Phoebe—we shall meet again, but not at the Café at the corner of the street ! *(Exits. Re-Enters after pause.)* Bah ! *(Exits double doors L.)*
(JEREMIAH knocks his bowler hat off as though in fright. It falls C. He puts TONY'S top hat on from table L. PHOEBE and JEREMIAH tremble.)
PHOEBE : (R.) Oh, Jerry—what will become of us ?
JEREMIAH : (L.) I wonder what they do to you over here ? *(He takes TONY'S top hat off and replaces it on the table L. and walks C. Picks up his own hat. He holds it above his head and shakes it—and his head—at the same time.)*
PHOEBE : Don't tremble so, Jerry.
JEREMIAH : I'm not trembling. I'm trying to find my head to put my hat on ! I'm a Quaker doing a bit of quaking ; that is, I'm quivering with rage. You know, it's just as well he's gone— another minute and I should have—*(Twists his hands as though screwing LAROSE'S neck)*.
PHOEBE : Take care, Jerry, he may come in at another door.
(Collapse of JEREMIAH, sits on chair R. of table L.)
JEREMIAH : Don't do it, Phoebe—you—you only frighten yourself.
(He shakes the chair under him as though he can't control his shaking, then puts his elbow on table and bangs it up and down.)
PHOEBE : I'll go and warn the Princess and finish the packing. *(Going to R.1.E.).*

JEREMIAH :	Yes, and I'll look out for the limp. (*Going L.1.E.*)
PHOEBE :	(*Comes back to R.C.*). Jerry ! ! (JEREMIAH *jumps as he hears his name.*) Don't be too fierce and get yourself into trouble. (*Going to R.1.E.*) because I do llke you a little.
JEREMIAH :	Oh Phoebe, you do—a little ? This is so sudden—I've come all of a tizwaz. (*Exits L.1.E.* PHOEBE *Exits R.1.E.*) (*Enter* MATHILDE *and* CHARTERIS *from R.2.E.*).
CHARTERIS :	Oh Mathilde, darling, it's wonderful to see you again after all these months. (*Moves to L.C. embracing.*)
MATHILDE :	Yes, and we're never going to part again, are we ?
CHARTERIS :	No, never. (*By this time they have walked to C. down stage and are embracing.* CHARTERIS *has his back to* BLUM *as she enters R.1.E., gesticulating despairingly.*)
BLUM :	Are we to do no more work at the Maison Blum ? (*Going down L.C.*) The Police are after my Princess—the Prince after my Quaker girl—Oh, these children ! (*To* CHARTERIS) Monsieur, it is impossible for you to be here.
CHARTERIS :	(*L.C., laughing*) Ah, but you see I am here ! We are going back to Barbizon.
BLUM :	You cannot, I tell you. The police watch Barbizon.
MATHILDE :	(*To* CHARTERIS) Nothing can happen now you have come back.
CHARTERIS :	Nothing. (*Embrace.*)
BLUM :	Oh, if I could only tell you in English, what I think of you in French. (PHOEBE *Enters R.1.E.* JEREMIAH *Enters L.1.E.*)
PHOEBE :	Everything's packed, madame.
JEREMIAH :	Where are you going, Phoebe ?
PHOEBE :	To Barbizon. (*Crosses L.*)
ALL :	To Barbizon ! To Barbizon !

No. 18.—MARCH QUINTET : (MATHILDE, PHOEBE BLUM, CHARTERIS and JEREMIAH.)
" Barbizon "
(*Marching movements ad lib. throughout the Number. See Dance Plot.*)

MATHILDE : (*C.*) Away together,
In lovers' weather,
To have our joyous June
Honeymoon !

CHARTERIS :	(C.)	In forest alleys
		And grassy valleys
		  We'll lead the simple life,
		  Little wife !

PHOEBE :	(To C.)	I'm simply chuckling
		To feed a duckling
		  And meet a tree that's not
		  In a pot.

JEREMIAH :	(To C.)	I'd give my wages
		For all the ages
		  To see a meadow now,
		  And a cow.

BLUM :		Oh, it feels so good When you wander in the wood.

ALL :		Away to balmy Barbizon !
		For such a happy time we'll go,
		  And have a cottage where
		  Our chanticleer
		At three a.m. will crow !
		Away in balmy Barbizon,
		  The breezes play a gay chanson.
		  And little lambs afar
		  Will echo ev'ry bar
		In Barbi-Barbizon !

MATHILDE :		It will be pleasant
		To play a peasant,
		  And live on curds and cream—
		  What a dream !

CHARTERIS :		And I my charmer,
		Will be the farmer,
		  In clumpy wooden shoes,
		  And a bloose.

PHOEBE :		I'll look my smartest,
		To catch an artist.
		  I'll show him if I ain't
		  Fit to paint !

JEREMIAH :		I'll take my chances
		At village dances,
		  And do dare-devil things
		  On the swings !

BLUM :		Oh, we'll laugh all day As we tumble in the hay !

ALL :		Away to balmy Barbizon !
		For such a happy time we'll go,
		  And have a cottage where
		  Our chanticleer
		At three a.m. will crow,

>   Away in balmy Barbizon,
>   The breezes play a gay chanson,
>   And little lambs afar
>   Will echo ev'ry bar.
>   In Barbi-Barbizon !

(DANCE *and Exeunt* R.1.E.)

(*Enter* PRINCE CARLO, *at double doors, meeting* TOINETTE *who Enters* R.1.E.—*puts bowl of flowers on table R.*)

PRINCE : (*Taking* TOINETTE *by the chin*) Ah, Toinette—Madame will allow you all to come to the dance, I hope ?

TOINETTE : (*R.*) It is too good of your Highness.

PRINCE : No, no, of *you*.

(DIANE *Enters* L.1.E.)

PRINCE : A dance would be rather tame without pretty girls, Toinette. (*Turns L. and sees* DIANE) Diane ! More charming than ever. (*To C.*)

DIANE : (*L.*) Ah, Prince, you also have come to see this Quaker girl—of course.

(TOINETTE *Exits* R.1.E.)

PRINCE : (*C.*) I have come to bring invitations to a little supper and dance. May I hope you will come too ?

DIANE : Is the Quaker girl to be there ? (*Crosses over to R.*)

PRINCE : I hope so.

DIANE : Thanks, then I *will* ! (*Sits on chair L. of table R.*)

PRINCE : (*Smiles*) Diane, it would please me more if this Mr. Chute were not so much in evidence—hein ?

DIANE : (*R.*) Ha, ha ! I will take care of Mr. Chute. (*Takes a packet of letters tied with red ribbon from her handbag*). Some of his letters to me.

PRINCE : Ah, I see. I suppose they will fall accidentally into the hands of the Quaker girl. (*Smiles*) Are they very— ?

DIANE : (*Offers them to him*) Judge for yourself.

PRINCE : No, no, no ! It is your affair ! (*She opens bag to replace the letters, He thus sees the contents*). You have quite a collection—are mine there ?

DIANE : (*Laughing*) Ha, ha ! Oh, yes, yours *and* Duhamel's. (*Produces a packet similar to the other, but tied with blue ribbon*) Ha, ha ! Duhamel in love ! But these are not for the little Quaker girl. (*Replaces them in bag.*)

PRINCE : Oh I see. (*Crosses to L.*) I trust, mamselle, you will have the success—you deserve ! A ce soir ?

DIANE : (*R*). A ce soir ! (PRINCE *bows and Exits* L.1.E.) (*Calling*) Toinette !

TOINETTE : Mamselle ! (*Entering* R.1.E.)

DIANE :	My new gown—is it ready ?
TOINETTE :	It is in the fitting room, mamselle.
DIANE :	It is a present from my friend, Mr. Chute. Ah, I hope it will fit.
TOINETTE :	I hope so, m'selle.
DIANE :	I wonder if that Quaker girl would let me see how it looks on her. She is about my height !
TOINETTE :	Oh, I'm sure she would, mamselle.
DIANE :	She is a mannequin here, is she not ?
TOINETTE :	Oui, mamselle.
DIANE :	Say it is for one of your best customers—you need not say who. Oh, and Toinette, there is a handbag to match the gown—is there not ?
TOINETTE :	Oui, mamselle.
DIANE :	Then would you be kind enough to put these in the handbag for me ? (*Gives* TOINETTE, *as she thinks,* CHUTE'S *letters, but really* DUHAMEL'S).
TOINETTE :	Certainly, mamselle. (*Exits R.1.E.*)
	(DIANE *sits on chair L. of table R. Enter* TONY, *L.1.E. He is rather taken aback at seeing* DIANE *but recovers himself. Picks up hat stick and gloves from table L. and tiptoes to door C.*)
DIANE :	Tony, where are you going ?
	(TONY *stops in his tracks as he hears her voice.*)
TONY :	I wasn't going anywhere, I was coming back ! (*Walking backwards to down C.*) Oh, by the way—I've ordered something for your neck.
DIANE :	A rope of pearls ?
TONY :	No, just the rope.
DIANE :	And now you have come to see the gown you are giving me ?
TONY :	Yes, yes ! But wouldn't it be better to have it sent to your home ?
DIANE :	I never wear a gown until I have seen it on one of the girls here ; it gives me so much better an idea of it.
TONY :	Now there I disagree with you. How could one of Blum's girls wear it with the distinction you would ? I ask you.
	(*He gets up and behind* DIANE, *threatens her with walking stick. She turns and sees him and he pretends to play violin, moving to C.*),
DIANE :	What are you hopping about for like a cat on hot bricks ?
TONY :	I've got cold feet, Diane. (*Goes to table L.*)
	(TOINETTE *Enters R.2.E. and Exits R.2.E. on* PRUDENCE'S *entrance*).
TOINETTE :	M'selle is ready. (*Pointing to R.C.*)

DIANE:	(*Rises, Crosses C.*) Ah! now. If you sit there— (*Indicating a point down L.C.*) you'll get the best idea of the effect.
TONY:	(*Coming down*) Oh no—you sit here, Diane.
DIANE:	Oh, no! I'll stand over there! (*Indicating R. upstage C.*)
TONY:	Oh you martyr!
DIANE:	I want to see the effect on you. (*Moves up L.C.*)
TONY:	But I'm not going to wear it. (*Sits on chair R. of table L. with his back to C.*)
	(TONY *does not immediately turn to see the costume.* PRUDENCE *Enters R.2.E. in* DIANE'S *costume, and comes down C., a la Mannequin.* DIANE *maliciously enjoying the situation.* PRUDENCE *forces herself to self-control.*)
DIANE:	(*L.C.*) Well?
TONY:	(*Rises*) Oh, I say, Diane, this is going too far. (*Rises and moves over to* PRUDENCE'S *L.*)
DIANE:	You mean it's too expensive. Oh, I've never known you consider the cost of a present to me before.
TONY:	(*L. of* PRUDENCE) I hope you don't think I had any hand in this?
PRUDENCE:	(*C.*) In what?
TONY:	This insult to you. (*Indicating* DIANE).
PRUDENCE:	Insult? I don't understand. Mamselle orders a gown— I am asked to put it on. It seems quite natural.
DIANE:	You find it quite comfortable?
PRUDENCE:	Yes, madame.
DIANE:	Perhaps you would walk a little.
	(TONY *exhibiting indignation as* PRUDENCE *moves up stage C. and back to down stage R.C.*)
TONY:	(*To* PRUDENCE) Don't walk. Oh, this is the limit. (*Crossing into C. Moves over to D/L.*)
DIANE:	(*L. to* TONY) The gown is smart enough, but, of course, as you said, it lacks distinction as this girl wears it. (*Moves over to* PRUDENCE'S *L.*) Sit down, and let me see how it looks.
TONY:	(*To* DIANE) Sit down yourself! (*To* PRUDENCE) Don't you sit down!
PRUDENCE:	But why not? Since mamselle desires it—and my duty permits? (*Sits R.C. on chair L. of table R.*)
DIANE:	(*L.C.*) Oh, don't sit so awkwardly, girl!
PRUDENCE:	I regret that not having had the training of an actress as mamselle has, I do the gown less than justice.
TONY:	(*C., aside to* PRUDENCE) Good girl! Good girl! You asked for that, Diane. (*Moving to C. on* PRUDENCE'S *L.*)

DIANE :	After all—(*Crosses R. to* PRUDENCE) I don't think I care much for it. You may get up, girl. (PRUDENCE *rises.* DIANE *looks at* PRUDENCE *again.*) No, I don't like it. (*To* TONY, *L.C.*) Perhaps you will let me give it to the girl for her trouble, and let me choose something else as a present. (*She squeezes* TONY'S *right hand*) I suppose I shall see you as usual at the theatre tonight ? (*She walks over to R.1.E.*)
TONY :	(*R.*) Not if I see you first.
DIANE :	(*Looking at* TONY) Tell the Quaker girl she may read what she finds in the handbag. (*Exits R.1.E.*)
	(PRUDENCE *sinks into chair, sobbing quietly.*)
TONY :	(*Coming over to* PRUDENCE, *R.C.*) Don't cry, I can't bear to see you cry !
PRUDENCE :	(*Sits up on chair*) Cry ! I'm not going to cry.
TONY :	You are — swell. Absolutely swell.
PRUDENCE :	(*L.*) Do you think a jealous woman is going to make me cry ?
TONY :	She knows I love you, Prudence. She knows I can think of no one else since I met you.
PRUDENCE :	(*Sweetly—sincerely—looking him earnestly in the eyes.*) Thee is speaking the truth, Tony ? No ! Don't answer me ! I believe thee ! All that—(*Indicating* DIANE) was before I knew thee ?
TONY :	Ever since I met you I have thought of no one but you, You *do* believe me, in spite of anything they may say ?
PRUDENCE :	In spite of everything ?
TONY :	There's something in the bag she meant you to find. (*He moves up and behind table R.C. to its R. facing* PRUDENCE.)
PRUDENCE :	What ? (*Takes out packet*) These ?
TONY :	My letters written to that lady before I knew you.
PRUDENCE :	Then please take them.
TONY :	(*Taking letters*) She's made a mistake—these are not mine
PRUDENCE :	Not yours ?
TONY :	No ! Mine were tied with red ribbon. I recognise the writing. They are from Monsieur Duhamel, the Minister, though he was for the high jump too !
PRUDENCE :	(*Takes letters. Crosses to L.C.*) Oh, then I'll return them to him myself—such a charming old gentleman.
TONY :	(*To her*) Prudence, it isn't true you're going to the Ball, is it ?
PRUDENCE :	Does thee not want me to, Tony ?
TONY :	No—it is not where I would like to see—my future wife.
PRUDENCE :	Then I won't go—Tony.
TONY :	You promise me ?

PRUDENCE :	I promise thee!
TONY :	Oh, Prudence—(*Going to embrace her, but she, shy, crosses R.*)
PRUDENCE :	I must see the Princess and tell her. I shouldn't have known you but for her.
TONY :	Prudence, we haven't once (*Indicating kiss—she walks slowly to* TONY, *offering her forehead*) No, not in the Quaker way. (*He kisses* PRUDENCE—*and she backs slowly a few paces, then turns and runs off R.1.E.*) Oh, I must go and find Charteris. I want to arrange about the furniture—(*He runs over to table L., picks up hat, gloves and stick and Exits L.1.E.*)
	(*The* WORK GIRLS *re-enter R.3.E. and busy themselves with the models in various ways.* TOINETTE *follows them on and gets L. in charge of them all.*)
TOINETTE :	(*L.*) We have lost time today—(*She indicates that she is bustling up the girls*)—and I don't know what to wear at the Prince's Ball to-night.
	(JEREMIAH'S *head only appears in opening R.2.E. looking into the room; when he sees the* GIRLS *his face beams—he doesn't come in, but speaks with his head showing.*)
JEREMIAH :	H'm! (ALL *the* GIRLS *look at him*). Excuse me, ladies, but would one of you be so kind as to sew a button on my—glove. (*Suddenly producing a white dress glove.*)
TOINETTE :	(*L/C.*) Monsieur Jeremiah! It is forbidden for you to enter here during working hours.
JEREMIAH :	Yes, I know—that's what I said to myself outside. I said, " Jerry, you mustn't go in, you *know* you mustn't go in." I said, " Mamselle Toinette will be so horribly angry (*Steps into the room*) at first. (*Another step*). And then she'll smile—showing those pretty teeth of hers— (TOINETTE *smiles, goes C.*) Yes, just like that—(*By this time he has got well into the room. The* GIRLS *do not crowd round him. The* GIRLS *form group around tables L. and R.*). Now, just think, how could I possibly amuse myself playing patience in the attic with all this loveliness on the ground floor. Won't you introduce me to the Duchesses? (*Indicating the* GIRLS).
TOINETTE :	The Duchesses—ha, ha! They are our Work Girls.
JEREMIAH :	I must get to work! (*Strolls over to the Mannequins L. To 5th Mannequin*) Ah, doing anything particular this evening?
5TH M.	We are always very particular about what we do in the evening.
	(*The* GIRLS *laugh at him.*)
JEREMIAH :	Ha, ha! Acid Drop Annie! I mean, couldn't we have a little lark?
GIRLS :	Lark?

JEREMIAH : (*Crosses R.*) Yes, let's go to the Bal Bullier—it'll only cost you a couple of million francs.
TOINETTE : (*Loftily*) The Bal Bullier! And pay for ourselves! We are going to the Pré Catalan to the Prince's Masked Ball.
JEREMIAH : (*Swaggering away R.*) Oh, is that tonight? I promised the Prince to look in—late. (*Moves over to R.C.*) I say, girls, you'll keep me a dance? (*Turning L.*)
TOINETTE : What about Mamselle Phoebe?
(PHOEBE, *unobserved, comes on R.2.E., crosses R. and sees the scene.* TOINETTE *mimes to* JEREMIAH *that* PHOEBE *is behind him.*)
JEREMIAH : Phoebe! Phoebe's all right! Don't wave to me! of course she's a trifle jealous of me—but there's no occasion to tell her everything we do, is there?
PHOEBE : (*R. coming forward*) No! (JEREMIAH *dives under apron*) Not a bit—when she can see for herself.
JEREMIAH : (*Crosses R.*) Phoebe, I was just trying to borrow a couple of Kirby grips! (*In front of table*).
PHOEBE : Yes, I know you were—I caught you at it.
TOINETTE : Ha, ha! The English girl is jealous. (*Goes D/L.*)
PHOEBE : (*Crosses L.C.*) Never mind whether I'm jealous or not— I want to know what you're doing with my young man.
TOINETTE : We are just improving him a little.
PHOEBE : He knew quite enough in our village—and I'm not going to have him improved here.
JEREMIAH : (*R.*) Now, now, don't quarrel about me.
PHOEBE : I might have known what would happen.
TOINETTE : (*C.*) You don't suppose we want that! (*Pointing to* JEREMIAH).
PHOEBE : Don't you talk like that of my Jeremiah—he's not much to look at, I know—
JEREMIAH : No—I know I'm not! What?
PHOEBE : —But he's too good for a lot of French Hussies.
TOINETTE : Hussies!
(*There is every indication of a row.*)
JEREMIAH : (*R.*) Phoebe, I wish you weren't quite so fond of me. (*Sits on* WORK GIRL'S *lap. He bends downand catches hold of a* WORK GIRL'S *legs who is sitting behind him. He apologises—and offers her the bowl of orchids from table.*)
PHOEBE : Fond of you, Jeremiah—I hate the very ground you walk on—but do you think I'm going to let these saucy French girls do as they like with you.
JEREMIAH : Wish you would!
TOINETTE : Mamselle l'Anglaise. (*Stamps foot*)

PHOEBE :   Well, Mamselle Francaise—(*Defiantly*)
                    (*They close in together C., preparing for a scrap.*)
JEREMIAH :   Please, please remember we're all ladies !
                    (*By this time the whole place is in a commotion—* JEREMIAH *gets in between* PHOEBE *and* TOINETTE *and gets the worst of it,* TOINETTE *throwing him to R.*
TOINETTE :   (*Up C.*) Pah ! Take away your Jeremiah. (*Crosses up L.*)
PHOEBE :   Yes, I will. I'll put him where he can't get into mischief.
                    (*Taking him by the ear to uppermost door of the fitting-room.*)
JEREMIAH :   Phoebe—if you'll let me explain. (*Standing in doorway*).
PHOEBE :   You get in there—I want to know where to find you when I come back.
JEREMIAH :   Phoebe—you're not going to lock me up.
PHOEBE :   I am ! The best place for you is under lock and key. (*Pushes him in*)
JEREMIAH :   (*Pops his head out of door*). Well, I shall make rude noises through the keyhole ! French ones ! ! (*Goes back again*)
                    (PHOEBE *locks door and comes down to C. with key.* GIRLS *laugh as they stroll R.3.E.* TOINETTE *remains.*)
PHOEBE :   You may laugh, but my Jerry's safe enough now ! (*Gets above R.1.E.*)
                    (*Enter* CHARTERIS *and* BLUM, *R.2.E. followed by* MATHILDE. MATHILDE *is the same as before ; i.e., as one of the* WORK GIRLS.)
CHARTERIS :   Come along ! I've a taxi all ready. (*Going up C.*)
                    (*Enter* LAROSE *C. He is followed by* TWO GENDARMES. ALL *still for tableau.* CHARTERIS *drops L. The* CHORUS *start entering in pairs from all entrances and group themselves around stage, leaving C. clear.*)

GENDARMES
O O

WORKGIRLS	PHOEBE			
O	O	BLUM	LAROSE	
MATHILDE		O	O	
				CHARTERIS
				O

LAROSE :   (*To* BLUM) Madame ! I have here a warrant for the arrest and deportation from France of Princess Mathilde.
                    (BLUM *moves down R. in front of* CHARTERIS *L. of table.*)
CHARTERIS :   (*L.C.*) Monsieur, the Princess Mathilde is now my wife.
LAROSE :   (*C., Smiles*) Monsieur refers to his marriage in England ?
CHARTERIS :   Certainly.

LAROSE :	Ah, Monsieur apparently does not know that such a marriage is not valid in France.
BLUM : CHARTERIS : }	Not valid ?
LAROSE :	No, monsieur, another marriage in France is necessary to make your union legal.
CHARTERIS :	Do you mean to tell me my wife is not my wife ?
LAROSE :	In France, monsieur, the Princess Mathilde is still unmarried.
BLUM :	Three days' honeymoon and only half married ! Oh ! (*Faints on armchair R.*)
PHOEBE :	(*Who has the key of the fitting room*) Oh, she's fainted. Something cold down her back—ah, the key ! (*Drops key seemingly down her back*).
CHARTERIS :	Monsieur Larose, this is an outrage.
LAROSE :	(*Shrugs shoulders*) Will madame now be good enough to indicate to me the Princess Mathilde ? (*Producing notebook and pen.*)
BLUM :	No, monsieur—jamais ! jamais ! ! jamais ! ! ! (*Rises.*)
LAROSE :	Very well, madame. (*To Gendarmes*) Guard the doors. (*They go up to doors. To* WORK GIRLS.) Mamselles, this way, please. (*He indicates that they shall come to his L. which they do one by one. He notes their names as they pass over to his L. and form a diagonal line.* (*To* TOINETTE) Your name ?
TOINETTE :	Toinette Lecouvreur !
LAROSE :	(*To* 1st GIRL) Yours ?
1st GIRL :	Marie la Grande.
MATHILDE :	Josephine Laronne.
2nd GIRL :	Mimi Dupont : (WORK GIRLS *form diagonal line down stage L.* BLUM, *R., restrains* CHARTERIS *from making any movement.* LAROSE *looks enquiringly at the* GIRLS, *then notices the doors of the fitting rooms, L.*)
LAROSE :	(*To* GENDARMES) Search those rooms !
GENDARME :	This door is locked, monsieur.
LAROSE :	Ah, locked ! At last ! Madame—the key !
PHOEBE :	(*Aside to* BLUM) Down your back ! (*Looks alarmed for* JEREMIAH.) (BLUM *shakes herself*).
LAROSE :	The key, madame ! Give me the key !
BLUM :	(*Shakes herself again before speaking*) Monsieur, it is not convenient.

LAROSE : Perhaps not, madame, but I insist! (*To* GENDARMES) Burst the lock.

PHOEBE : (*Rushing to R. of* LAROSE) Oh, please Mr. Chief of Police!

LAROSE : (*To* PHOEBE) The Princess is in there—(*Pushes* PHOEBE *away up stage*)—burst the lock.

(*The lock is burst with comic business by the* GENDARMES. JEREMIAH *emerges and walks down C.* PHOEBE *crosses to the rescue of* JEREMIAH. MATHILDE, TOINETTE *and the* WORK GIRLS *are L.*)

JEREMIAH : (*Dressed as woman*) I now declare the Bazaar open!

LAROSE : (*Furious, to* GENDARMES) Take him away! (*They go to seize* JEREMIAH.)

PHOEBE : (*Spinning the big* GENDARME *over*) You leave my Jerry alone. Push the little one over, Jerry.

(JEREMIAH *does so, then they take arms and both sing* " Britons never, never, never shall be slaves " *and march off at double doors.*)

LAROSE : Sacrebleu! (*Going down L.*)

(ALL *laugh at* LAROSE'S *discomfiture.* BLUM *and* CHARTERIS *are R.C.*

No.19.—FINALE

(*For movements see Dance Plot*)

CHORUS OF GIRLS :
Ah, ha, Monsieur Larose!
   We honour and admire you.
But must suggest your taking a rest,
   Your noble work must tire you!
And though our window shows
   The very latest dresses,
We haven't got a suitable lot
   Of runaway Princesses!
We'll get you some
   If you propose
Again to come,
   Monsieur Lacrose—

(LAROSE *goes up and consults with* GENDARMES.)

Ah, ha, Monsieur Larose.
   We'll show her,
   When we know her,
Ah, ha, ha, ha, ha, ha, aha, ah, ha,
   Monsieur Larose!

(LAROSE *goes up stage* PRUDENCE, *enters from L.1.E.* MATHILDE *goes up to meet* PRUDENCE *and brings her L.C.*).

MATHILDE :   (*R. to* PRUDENCE)
  Oh, there's Monsieur Larose,
    The man that I detested,
  He says I'm here, he knows,
    And I must be arrested.
  And if he catches me,
    Our marriage won't be lawful,
  And never more can be—
    The case is simply awful !
  Oh, what are we to do   (BLUM *moves up C.*
  If it's true, —if it's true. —*looking off R.*).
    Our honeymoon
    Is over soon,
  And what are we to do ?
    (MATHILDE *moves back to L. with other* WORK GIRLS
    CHARTERIS *moves up to meet* LAROSE *and comes down
    C. with him, with* BLUM *on his L.*)

CHARTERIS :   (*Angrily, crossing to* LAROSE)
  Pardon, Monsieur Larose,
    But did I hear it truly,
  You venture to suppose
    We are not married duly ?

LAROSE :   Again I must declare
    Your marriage to be legal
  Must here be by a Mayor,
    If not, you know the sequel !

CHARTERIS :   (*Speaks*) But, monsieur !

LAROSE :   (*Speaks*) It is the law.
    (CHARTERIS *turns his back on* LAROSE.)
    (*If preferred* LAROSE *and* GENDARMES *may exit up staircase
    R. and a cut be made to page 167 of vocal Score.*)

MATHILDE : ⎫
PRUDENCE : ⎬   Then what are we to do
CHARTERIS : ⎭   If it's true, if it's true ?
  (My)   (I)
  (Your) own sweetheart and (you) must part,
  And what are we to do ?

PRUDENCE :   Although Monsieur Larose
    At present hasn't found you,
  You have too many foes
    All on the watch around you.
  If we could only find
    A way by which to save you,
  Not one of us would mind
    If life and all we gave you.

MATHILDE : ⎫
PRUDENCE : ⎬   But what are we to do
CHARTERIS : ⎭   If it's true, if it's true ?
    It's all too late to conquer fate,
  So what are we to do ?

CHORUS OF GIRLS :	(*Bowing* LAROSE *off*) Adieu, Monsieur Larose, You grieve us When you leave us ! Ah, ah, ah, ah, ah, ah, ah, ah ! Monsieur Larose. (LAROSE *Exits C. doors followed by* GENDARMES. BLUM *signs to* MATHILDE *to join* WORK GIRLS *up L. She does so. The* PRINCE *Enters R.2.E. The* FULL CHORUS *is now on stage, informally grouped.*)
CHORUS MAN :	(*Looking off stage R.I.E.*) Madame ! The Prince !
ALL :	The Prince ! The Prince ! His Highness ! (ALL *curtsey*.)
PRINCE :	(*C. to* BLUM *on his L.*) Ah, Madame, Here I am To invite La Quakeress ! (*Kisses* BLUM'S *hand*) (*To* PRUDENCE *C., on his L.*) May I pray You will say As your answer, only " Yes "? (PRUDENCE *crosses over to his R.*) Will you not come to the ball ? Listen and answer the call, Beautiful girls will be there to dance, All that are fairest and best in France. If you will come to the ball, You shall be Queen of them all, No one so fair will be there At the ball, at the ball !
PRUDENCE : :	Really, your Highness, Though you are kind, Quakerish shyness Troubles my mind. I am no dancer, I cannot go, So I can answer Nothing but no ! (PRUDENCE *moves over to* BLUM, *R.C., The* PRINCE *endeavours to persuade her, but she politely declines.* PRUDENCE *and* BLUM *walk up stage C.*)
CHORUS :	Her only answer is " No." She will not come to the ball, She will not answer the call. (*The* PRINCE *walks up stage C. and brings* BLUM *downstage on his left hand and* PRUDENCE *on his right hand.*)

ENSEMBLE

PRINCE : Ah ! Ah !
She will not come to the ball,
Then I'll make love to them all.
Many as fair will be there
At the ball, at the ball !
CHORUS : If she would come to the ball
She would be Queen of us all,
She does not care to be there
At the ball, at the ball !

(CHARTERIS *moves down R.*)

(PRINCE *leads* PRUDENCE *R.* LAROSE *and* GENDARMES *return through double doors, down to* PRINCE'S *L.* BLUM *is R., looking at* MATHILDE.)

(*Dialogue during Music.*)

LAROSE : (*L. of* PRINCE) Your Highness, I ask your assistance in the name of the law.
PRINCE : (*L.C.*) Certainly, Larose—but how ?
LAROSE : The Princess Mathilde—to whom your Highness was betrothed, is here.
PRINCE : The Princess Mathilde here ?
LAROSE : Here, amongst these girls. (*Indicating Girls L.*) I ask you to identify her. (*Goes down L.*)
PRUDENCE : (*R.C., aside to* PRINCE) No, no !
PRINCE : Ah, but mamselle, you refuse to come to the Ball ?
PRUDENCE : I am sorry, monsieur, but I—I cannot.
PRINCE : (*Shrugging his shoulders*) Then—I see no reason for refusing to do as Larose asks.

(PRUDENCE, *agitated, stands R.C. as the* PRINCE *crosses to* GIRLS *L. On reaching* MATHILDE *he pauses significantly in dead silence ; he then addresses* PRUDENCE, *who is R.C.*)—Well ?

PRUDENCE : I will go to the Ball !
PRINCE : Ah ! (*He now turns up stage to* LAROSE *down L.*) The Princess Mathilde is not here, Monsieur.

(LAROSE *gives an exclamation of impatience and disappointment, bows and Exits with* GENDARMES *at double doors.*)

ENSEMBLE

PRINCE :
Ah ! You will come to the ball.
Listen and answer the call.
I will be ever your faithful friend,
You are my queen till the world shall end.
Now you will come to the ball
You shall be queen of them all.

PRUDENCE :
Yes, I will go to the ball,
Now I must answer the call.
If I have power to help my friend.
What do I care though the world may end ?
Yes, I will come to the ball,
Join in the dance with them all.

CHORUS AND OTHER PRINCIPALS :
Ah ! she will come to the ball,
Listen and answer the call.
Fair is the fate of the Prince's friend,
Queen of the dance to the dance's end.
Ah ! Let us come to the ball,
Hailing her Queen of us all !

(*During the latter part of this, the* PRINCE *offers his arm to* PRUDENCE *and walks her up and down stage from R. to L., at end of which she is on his L.*)

(*Enter* TONY *at double doors, and down L., he starts at seeing* PRUDENCE *on the arm of the* PRINCE.)

TONY :
(*L.*) Prudence, are you going to this Prince's Ball in spite of your promise to me ?

PRUDENCE :
Yes, but you don't understand—

TONY :
I understand enough to know I never want to see you again. (*Exit through double doors C.*)

PRUDENCE :
Tony ! ! !

(PRUDENCE *follows him up stage and stands looking after him off R.*)

PRINCE :
No one so fair will be there
At the Ball—at the Ball.

(PRINCE *goes to table R., picks up hat, stick, and stands in front of table R.*)

CHORUS :
Hail to the pair of them there,
At the Ball—at the Ball !

(PRUDENCE *runs up stage to C. doors, looking after* TONY.

CURTAIN.

ACT III

No. 20.—OPENING ACT III.
" Champagne ! "
(NOTE : THE CHORUS *need only sing* " Champagne "
*as it accurs in the music and omit the rest of the lyric.
This is how it was played in the London Revival.*)

1st HALF :	What is the wine ?
2nd HALF :	It comes from France.
1st HALF :	It tickles your spine
2nd HALF :	And makes you dance—
ALL :	Champagne !
GIRLS :	Champagne !
1st HALF :	Before you've thought
2nd HALF :	You start to sing ;
1st HALF	You're doing a sort
2nd HALF :	Of Haarlem Swing—
ALL :	Champagne !
GIRLS :	Mmm ! Mmm !
MEN :	Little Miss Debutante, be wise— Never be shy or dumb. When he says, " What'll— ? "
GIRLS :	The answers', " A Bottle Of Mum—Mum—Mum."
ALL :	Mum—Mum !
1st HALF :	It's full of the Spring,
2nd HALF :	It's full of the Sun ;
ALL :	A bubbly thing Of bubbly fun— That's Champagne.
1st GIRL :	When Charles the Second Was theatre mad, And Nellie beckoned Him round they had—
ALL :	Champagne !
GIRLS :	Champagne !
2nd GIRL :	When Pompadour with A roguish glance Had wiped the floor with The King of France—
ALL :	Champagne !
GIRLS :	Mmm ! Mmm !
3rd GIRL :	Henry the Eighth had sex appeal And something else, we know.

1st Man :	Sensible feller, For he had a cellar Of Veuve Cliquot Oh ! Oh !
4th Girl :	If only she'd seen A bottle of fizz There'd never have been A Good Queen Liz—
All :	That's Champagne !

(CHAMPAGNE BALLET—*see Dance Plot.*)

(*Enter* PRINCE *from L.2.E. with* DIANE *on his left arm.* TOINETTE *R.*)

PRINCE : (*C. to* TOINETTE) You will give me a dance, mamselle ? (*As they walk to R.C.*)

(DIANE *breaks L.*)

TOINETTE : (*R.*) With pleasure, monsieur—I love dancing.
PRINCE : And I also—with you for a partner.
DIANE : (*L.*) The Quaker girl has not yet arrived, Prince ?

(TOINETTE *crosses behind* PRINCE *to table L.*)

PRINCE : Not yet.
DIANE : Do you think she will keep her promise and come ?
PRINCE : Oh, yes(*To table L.*) she will be here. Her Mr. Chute is definitely out of favour and I intend to give her her first glimpse of real life, Diane.

(PRINCE *sits on table, C.* TOINETTE *on his R. on chair,* DIANE *on his L. on chair.*)

No. 21.—SONG : (PRINCE and CHORUS.)
" Couleur de Rose "

(*During the Symphony the guests all group over stage R. and L. ; some on the restaurant steps; for movements see Dance Plot.*)

PRINCE : The world's a delightful place,
And if you're fond of a gay time,
Fling care to the winds
And make up your minds
That all the year shall be May-time !
Away with your gloomy thoughts
Just do what fancy proposes
Then life ought to seem
A beautiful dream
A dream of nothing but roses !

Couleur de Rose ! Couleur de Rose !
That is what life should be.
Rosy cheeks may blush provokingly
Rosy lips may kiss you jokingly.
Laughter and song all the day long,
Echoing far and free.
Give me a world that glitters and glows,
Couleur de rose ! Couleur de rose !

Chorus :	Couleur de rose ! Couleur de rose ! etc.

Prince :	Philosophy such as mine
	  You mayn't believe till you've tried it.
	  But life is a cup
	  One ought to fill up,
	  And quaff the nectar inside it.
	Then, under a cloudless sky
	  With not a shadow of sorrow,
	  We'll learn, while we may,
	  The joys of today,
	  And leave regrets till tomorrow.
	Couleur de rose ! Couleur de rose ! etc.
	(The second verse may be omitted if desired).
	
	(During the Refrain the Guests *partnered move quietly over from L. and group on R. and C.* Prince, Toinette *and* Diane *pass U/S. and Exit R.2.E. After song* Larose *appears L.1.E. as though having made his way through the throng. The people on the stage laugh a little at* Larose. *at which he has some difficulty in restraining his annoyance. The* Guests *who address him are the* Mannequins *of Maison* Blum, *who come R. and L. of him.)*

1st Guest :	Look out ! ! The man with the limp !
2nd Guest :	Have you seen the evening papers, monsieur ? *(General laugh.* Guests *Exeunt at all sides, palpably laughing at* Larose, *who walks about in suppressed anger—he looks as though expecting someone—and gives a little ejaculation and gets L. as he sees* Duhamel *Enter R.U.E.* Blum *Enters from restaurant.)*
Larose :	*(Aside)* Pussy cats !
Blum :	Monsieur le Ministre, I have been looking everywhere for you. *(As She and* Duhamel *descend steps)*
Larose :	*(Bowing stiffly)* Madame.
Blum :	Monsieur. (Larose *Exits stiffly L.U.E.* Phoebe *and* Toinette *Re-enter from restuurant and stand on restaurant steps)* Oh, Monsieur le Ministre ! *(Crosses C.)* What a lovely party—the music—the champagne. It makes me feel so good. Are you in a good mood ?
Duhamel :	Always with you, madame.
Blum :	Bien. Then I want to ask a favour—a great favour—you will not send my little Princess away—until she is properly married ?
Duhamel :	Madame !
Blum :	Ah Monsieur—just think—three days' honeymoon— and only half married.

DUHAMEL :	I regret, madame, I can do nothing. (*Crosses L.*) The Princess must leave France.
BLUM :	(*Sees* TOINETTE *coming down on her R., accompanied by* PHOEBE) Go, Toinette—and see what you can do !
TOINETTE :	I'll go and dance with him. He likes that much better, madame. You get the little Quaker girl to coax him. (*Exits with* DUHAMEL, L.1.E.)
BLUM :	The Quaker girl ! Good ! I forget—yes ! She is in the restaurant. (*Crosses to* PHOEBE *R.*) Wait here, Phoebe— I go to find the little Prudence. (*Exits into restaurant.*)

(*Enter* JEREMIAH *with* TWO GIRLS, *L.2.E.*)

JEREMIAH :	Oh what a night !—what a party ! (*Smacks one girl on stomach before seeing* PHOEBE.)

(GIRLS *run off L.2.E.*)

PHOEBE :	(*R.C.*) Jerry—why must I always find you with your arm round some other girl's waist ?
JEREMIAH :	(*L.*) It's this place, Phoebe, and that bubbly stuff ; my arms keep getting a curve on them. Look at this one ! Waiting for you, Phoebe. (*Places his arm round her waist*)
PHOEBE :	I don't think you've behaved at all nicely to me since we've been here.
JEREMIAH :	Then I'll make up for it as soon as we get away.
PHOEBE :	Do you really like me better than any of those French girls ?
JEREMIAH :	Of course—and Phoebe—
PHOEBE :	Yes ?
JEREMIAH :	I'll buy you anything you want, when we really get on in the world.

No. 22.—DUET: (JEREMIAH and PHOEBE)
" Mr. Jeremiah Esquire "

PHOEBE :	(*L.*)	When we are really rich, Then married we will get ;
JEREMIAH	(*R.*)	We'll settle down Somewhere in Town Among the swagger set.
PHOEBE :		A house in Berkeley Square Will be our new Address ;
JEREMIAH		We'll dine in state Off silver plate With spoons from L.M.S.
BOTH :		Spoons *and* forks from L.M.S.

PHOEBE :	Oh Jerry,
	Will you pass the Sherry ?
	Kindly bid the butler stir the fire.

JEREMIAH :	That's the sort of thing we'll say
	On that happy, happy day
	When I'm Mr. Jeremiah Esquire.

PHOEBE :	We'll join the " Upper Ten,"
	Most frightfully well-bred ;

JEREMIAH	With you and me
	They'll have to be
	The " Upper Twelve " instead.

PHOEBE :	I'll bath myself in milk
	With showers of " Chanel " ;

JEREMIAH :	And I'll have mine
	In brandy wine—
	And drink it up as well !

PHOEBE :	Oh, Jerry !
	You can call me " Cherie,"
	I shall curtsey down and call you " Sire."

JEREMIAH :	I'll be privileged to smack
	Lady Astor on the back,
	When I'm Mr. Jeremiah Esquire.
	(*Dance see Dance Plot. Exeunt L. I. E.*)

PHOEBE :	We'll have a country house
	As big as an hotel

JEREMIAH :	Insist upon
	" With all mod. con.
	And Offices as well."

PHOEBE :	We'll hunt and shoot and fish
	As tweed-y as can be ;

JEREMIAH :	A hunting suit
	So I can shoot
	Welsh-Rarebits for my tea.

BOTH :	Big Welsh-Rarebits for our tea.

PHOEBE :	Oh, Jerry
	We'll be very merry—
	Quite the gayest couple in the Shire.

JEREMIAH	And perhaps with perfect ease
	We'll have one—two—
PHOEBE :	Jerry, please !

JEREMIAH :	When you're Mrs. Jeremiah Esquire.
	(*Dance.*)

	(*Encore Verse*)

PHOEBE :	With social life alone
	You'll never be content,

JEREMIAH :	So by and bye I'll have a try To enter Parliament.
PHOEBE :	When you begin to talk The world will be surprised ;
JEREMIAH :	And folks may feel My sex appeal If I get televised.
BOTH :	Oh $\left\{\begin{array}{c}\text{you'll}\\ \text{I'll}\end{array}\right\}$ look lovely televised !
POEBE :	Oh, Jerry ! I should think you're very Likely to set Parliament on fire.
JEREMIAH :	And my speeches every night Will be broadcast, Home and Light, When I'm M.P. Jeremiah, Esquire ! (*Dance*)
PHOEBE :	Oh, Jerry ! Bevan they can bury, You're the sort of statesman we require.
JEREMIAH :	And the Duke will tell the Queen Now the future's all serene, We've got Mr. Jeremiah, Esquire !

(*Both Exit L. down stage entrance*)

(*Enter* PRUDENCE, MATHILDE *and* CHARTERIS *from restaurant.*)

PRUDENCE :	(*C.*) You're not going to leave me here alone, are you ?
MATHILDE :	(*L.*) Of course not—we will take care of you.
CHARTERIS :	(*R.*) Why, but for you, my wife might now be under arrest.
PRUDENCE :	(*C.*) I have come to this Ball because I said I would—but I won't stay.
CHARTERIS :	I have heard that Monsieur Duhamel is to be here.
PRUDENCE :	Monsieur Duhamel—the Minister—who was so nice to me today ?
CHARTERIS :	Yes, I'm going to ask him to let the Princess stay long enough in France for us to get married again.
PRUDENCE :	He told me I might ask any favour of him. (*Moves over to* MATHILDE'S *R.*)
CHARTERIS : MATHILDE :	Did he ?
PRUDENCE :	Yes ! (*Suddenly remembering*) Oh, and I have something to give him. (*Producing the packet of letters tied with blue ribbon*)

(*Enter* PRINCE *L. from Restaurant.*)

	You will see everything will come right for you—(*Moves behind* CHARTERIS *to R.C.*) As for me, I'm afraid Tony will never forgive me for coming here.
PRINCE :	Ah, mamselle, at last—a thousand times welcome ! (*He goes to* PRUDENCE'S *R.*)
PRUDENCE :	(*R.C.*) Monsieur, I have come as I promised. But—
PRINCE :	(*R.*) But since you are here, mamselle, come and see my poor efforts to entertain you. (*Offers his arm to* PRUDENCE *and turns up stage with her, remaining on, in conversation.*)
MATHILDE :	(*L.C.*) We mustn't leave Prudence too much alone with the Prince.
CHARTERIS :	(*Moves behind* MATHILDE *to her R.*) We must go and find Duhamel. Everything depends on him.
	(MATHILDE *and* CHARTERIS *Exit L.1.E., hand in hand.*)
PRINCE :	(*Coming down R.C. with* PRUDENCE *on his R.*) Well, mamselle, I hope you'll like the Ball.
PRUDENCE :	Oh, it must be lovely being a Prince.
PRINCE :	For me there has never before been an evening like this, mamselle. You will give me the first dance ?
PRUDENCE :	Quakers don't dance, monsieur. (*Breaks D/R.*)
PRINCE :	Then at least Quakers sup, I suppose ?
PRUDENCE :	(*Laughing*) Oh, sometimes, but not as Princes do.
	(*Enter* MADAME BLUM *from restaurant.*)
PRINCE :	I have a table over there (*Indicating L.*) where we shall be alone. (*Offering his arm*).
BLUM :	I don't think ! (*Coming down stage R.*)
PRUDENCE :	Oh, Madame Blum ! (*Rushing to her. Moves down R. to* PRINCE.) If you will let me join you in a moment or two.
PRINCE :	Certainly, mamselle. I shall await you with impatience. (*Bows and Exits with* TWO GIRLS *L.2.E.*)
BLUM :	He is coming this way, the Minister, you will ask him to let the Princess stay ? (*She has seen* DUHAMEL *approaching L.1.E.*)
PRUDENCE :	Of course I will.
BLUM :	Good ! Good ! He must not see me. You know, you bring good fortune, my little Quaker girl. Ah, you bring luck, I know. He must not see me, so I will run, cherie. (*Exit through restaurant R.*)
	(*Enter* DUHAMEL *L.1.E.*)
DUHAMEL :	(*L.*) Ah, mamselle, I have been looking everywhere for you.
PRUDENCE :	(*R.*) And I have been looking for you, monsieur. (*To R.C.*)
DUHAMEL :	(*Very flattered*) Indeed ! (*Moving to C.*).

PRUDENCE :	I want to ask you something—something you have refused others, monsieur.
DUHAMEL	So much the better. It will prove I can refuse you nothing !
PRUDENCE :	Then please, please let my friend the Princess remain in France.
DUHAMEL :	Mamselle, I beg you to ask me anything but that.
PRUDENCE :	But there is nothing else I have to ask, monsieur.
DUHAMEL :	Then I regret—(*Turns away*).
PRUDENCE :	(*Pause*) Monsieur, I have some letters—they are yours, I think. (*Shows the packet*).
DUHAMEL :	(*L., starting in surprise*) My letters ! May I ask where you obtained them ?
PRUDENCE :	From the lady to whom they are addressed, monsieur.
DUHAMEL :	From Mamselle Diane ! Ah, I see, they were given to you to force me to consent to the Princess remaining at liberty in France. (*Bitterly*) And you would bribe me with them. Well, mamselle, I refuse. And now—what do you propose to do with them ?
PRUDENCE :	The letters, monsieur ? I only brought them here to return them to you. (*Offering them*).
DUHAMEL :	You give them to me without any condition ?
PRUDENCE :	Certainly, monsieur. Quakers do not traffic in such things !
DUHAMEL :	(*Taking them*) But—I have refused to grant your request.
PRUDENCE :	(*Simply, but sadly*) Yes, monsieur. Still I am happy to have been of any little service to you. That is all. (*Crosses R.*)
DUHAMEL :	(*C.*) Mamselle ! (*Takes* PRUDENCE'S *left hand*) Forgive my having misunderstood you. I will grant your request.
PRUDENCE :	(*Joyfully*) You will ? And the Princess may stay ?
DUHAMEL :	It shall be as you wish.
PRUDENCE :	Oh, monsieur, how can I ever thank you ?
DUHAMEL :	No thanks, my child, but think of your own happiness as well as that of others. Take care of the Prince. (*Moves up to restaurant on to steps.*)
PRUDENCE :	I do not think of the Prince, but of someone else.
DUHAMEL :	Mamselle, I understand. And please remember, I am still young enough for that. (*Exits into restaurant.*)
PRUDENCE :	Oh, I'm so happy, I should like to dance—as Tony taught me (*Crosses to table L.*)

No. 23.—SONG : (PRUDENCE)
" Tony from America "

PRUDENCE :	All along the garden where the moonbeams glance, Music echoes loud and clear. Girls have got their partners for the joyous dance, But the one I want's not here.

There are partners made in Germany,
And gentlemen of France,
There are boys who come from England, but
They haven't any chance
With
Tony, from America,
Over the sea !
He guessed I was all alone,
So that's why he came along and found me !
Over in America,
Some day we'll be,
When a cottage we have rented,
We'll be quite contented,
Tony and me !
All along the path way of the summer moon
He is coming now, I know.
He is out to find me and he'll meet me soon,
Whisper to me soft and low.
There are girls who blush and smile at him
And try to win his heart,
For they want him very badly, but
I never mean to part
With
Tony from America, etc.

(*Dance—See Dance Plot—Last* 8 *Bars of Second Dance Chorus sung*).
(PRUDENCE *finishes Number sitting on table down stage L.*).
(*Enter* TONY *from R.3.E.*)

PRUDENCE : Tony !
TONY : (*R., quietly but bitterly*) So, you are here—in spite of your promise ?
PRUDENCE : (*L., gently*) I was obliged to come, friend Tony.
TONY : (*Bitterly*) Obliged ! Obliged to break your word ! Why ? Because you are a woman ? (*Turns away to R.*)
PRUDENCE : (*Gently*) Thou dost not understand. (*Moves to R.C.*)
TONY : (*Walks down stage to R. of* PRUDENCE) Indeed I do !
PRUDENCE : Yet, if thou wilt listen.
TONY : (*Interrupting*) Listen ! The man who listens to a woman is a *fool*. You have fooled me once—and you will try to fool me again. And to think I trusted you. (*Crosses to behind* PRUDENCE).
PRUDENCE : (*Naively*) Is that why thou hast followed me here ?
TONY : I came here because I couldn't believe that you would break your word to me.
PRUDENCE : Thou hast doubts of me ?
TONY : Doubts ? I believe my own eyes. You are here—that's enough. You have pretended to love me—and you put yourself at the beck and call of the first man that flatters your vanity.

PRUDENCE :	(*Gently*) Thou dost not flatter me, friend. My coming here was the bribe I had to give the Prince. (*Moves to C.*)—to prevent his pointing out the Princess to the Chief of Police.
TONY :	(*Touched*) You did that—to serve her ?
PRUDENCE :	Verily. Was it too great a price to pay ? I did not think so—(*Looks back to* TONY, *walks away slowly to R.C.*)—until I tasted the bitterness of thy doubt of me. (*With feeling.*)
TONY :	(*Puts hat and stick on table down L. C., and walks over to* PRUDENCE'S *L.*) Forgive me. I go too quick ! I jump to conclusions. I'll improve—when I get—(*Takes* PRUDENCE'S *hands gently.*)
PRUDENCE :	(*Demurely*) Wisdom ?
TONY	No—Prudence !

No. 24.—DUET : (PRUDENCE and TONY).
" The First Dance "

PRUDENCE :	Thee loves me and I love thee,
	    Love's the only true marriage maker,
	Thy little wife I'm going to be,
	    And *not* the little wife of a Quaker.
	Though I have been asked by many,
	    It's true !

TONY :	Just take a step, take a step, take a step !
PRUDENCE :	I would never dance with any But you !
TONY :	Just take a step, take a step, take a step !
PRUDENCE :	All in vain the rest besought me Tonight !
TONY :	Just take a step, take a step, take a step !
PRUDENCE :	Now I'll do the dance you taught me—
BOTH	All right !
	(*Dance : that of No. 17 perfected—See Dance Plot.*)
	(*Enter* MATHILDE, *R. with* CHARTERIS, *from restaurant, and* PHOEBE *and* JEREMIAH *from L.1.E.*)
MATHILDE :	Prudence, have you seen Monsieur Duhamel ?
PRUDENCE :	Yes, and everything is all right.
TONY :	Charteris, I've fixed it up all right.
CHARTERIS :	Congratulations, my boy. (*Shakes hands*)
PHOEBE :	(*To* JEREMIAH) Now you and I can get married, Jerry !
JEREMIAH :	What, here ?
PHOEBE :	Nay, we'll go back to the village green.

JEREMIAH :	What after all this time in Paris ? We'll never be green again. (CHORUS *Enter here and form three lines across stage. Enter* PRINCE *and* DIANE *on his left arm—from L.2.E.* PRINCE *stands on* PHOEBE'S *L. Enter* BLUM *from restaurant.* DUHAMEL *enters L.*)
LAROSE :	(*Produces warrant. To* MATHILDE) Pardon, madame, voila !
DUHAMEL :	(*Drops R.*) The Princess was exiled. She is no longer a French subject. The English marriage was perfectly valid—even in France. (LAROSE *retires defeated to R. of* TOINETTE.)
BLUM :	Then the three days' honeymoon was all right. (*Crosses to R. of* TONY.) (ALL *cheer.*)

WARN CURTAIN.

(PRINCIPALS *in one line across stage.*)

No. 25.—FINALE.

TOIN ; LAROSE, MATH ; CHAR ; BLUM ; TONY, PRU ; JERRY, PHOE ; PRINCE, DIANE, DUH ;

PRUDENCE :	Love, I have met you and known you, Love, at your throne I adore. If you will stay, Be my life what it may, Mine will be joy evermore !
ALL :	Love, as our master we own you, Freely we answer your call ; And ours while we live. Be the joys that we give ; Love, you are lord of us all ! Love, you are lord of us all !
ALL Sing :—	1 Chorus " Come to the Ball " — 1st Curtain. 1 Chorus " Tony from America " — 2nd Curtain. 1 Chorus " Come to the Ball " — 3rd Curtain. 1 Chorus " Come to the Ball "—AS PLAY OUT.

CURTAIN.

END OF PLAY.

DANCE PLOT

No. 1. OPENING ACT I *Movements* :	JARGE C. Two semicircles GIRLS all round singing Opening Chorus. 3 MEN, 2 BOYS. Standing facing towards JARGE, hands on knees bending forward, back GIRLS coming forward into one semicircle, then returning to original positions, entrance of Mrs. LUKYN at Inn Door, GIRLS turning to Mrs. LUKYN, pointing. Mrs. LUKYN moving to stage C. VILLAGERS excited, listen to her as she chants, group round her, 3 kneeling on floor. VILLAGERS moving at end of dialogue to positions outside Meeting House and Inn Door, ALL exit on various cues.
No. 2. QUAKERS' ENTRANCE.	QUAKERS and QUAKERESSES enter from Quakers' House R.2.E. with slow stately walk into one line, facing front, GIRLS slightly forward movements with head and bend of knees. At Entrance of VILLAGERS, QUAKERS move to stage R. into two lines facing stage L.
VILLAGERS' ENTRANCE. " SOLOMON GRUNDY "	Run on in three lines from stage L. laughing, GIRLS all facing front, hands behind back, bobbing on words " Solomon Grundy." hands in front, chain movement round stage, stepping back to positions in three lines. Facing QUAKERS, movements are 8 paces, starting with L. foot from side to side 4 forward walks, turn on QUAKERS as they walk round in circle to original positions facing front. VILLAGERS stamping. facing front, bending forward, hands on knees, feet together, then R. Hands, head, and out to front, turning once to end of Refrain. QUAKERS move back to positions facing VILLAGERS who group round tree and outside Inn and exit on RACHEL'S line.
No. 3. " O, TIME, TIME !"	Commence song seated for Verse. On Refrain MATHILDE walks slowly to stage R. walks to C. and over to stage L. back again slowly to C. and over to R. walks back to C. and over to L. takes 3 paces back and 2 paces forward, on " Fly Away, Time, curtsey on L. at finish.
No. 4. " WONDERFUL."	CHARTERIS and MATHILDE embrace on entrance, hold hands C. stage, MATHILDE facing front CHARTERIS bows and goes R. after MATHILDE who walks to C. and both walk over to L. CHARTERIS shows MATHILDE form L.C., MATHILDE embraces, both take hands and walk back to C. finishing number both in curtsey.
No. 5. " A RUNAWAY MATCH."	TONY, PHOEBE and CHARTERIS turn to MATHILDE as she sings then TONY, PHOEBE and MATHILDE turn to CHARTERIS as he sings. At cue " Runaway Match " all hold hands and with R. foot first, gallop down stage. TONY, PHOEBE and MATHILDE on one knee facing CHARTERIS. At cue " Runaway Match " gallop down stage, R. foot first. At Refrain hold hands and skip sideways to stage L. then right across to stage R. Walk back to C. and gallop down, R. foot first. In 2nd verse MEN turn

	and walk up. PHOEBE sings to MATHILDE. ALL gallop down as before leaving TONY in front for his Verse. Refrain as before.
No. 8. "A BAD BOY AND A GOOD GIRL."	Dance : PRUDENCE jumps up, TONY, surprised, jumps after her. Repeat twice. Thinking PRUDENCE is going to dance, TONY shows her a tap step, but with disgust she walks to the cottage door. TONY runs after her and almost collides as she turns. PRUDENCE gives a deep curtsey. TONY kisses her and she runs off through cottage door. TONY kisses the doorpost, gate, etc.
No. 9. "TIP-TOE."	VILLAGERS enter, MEN standing back stage. GIRLS enter in twos from stage L. with movement from side to side, walking to positions in two lines facing stage R., marking time on spot, starting with L. foot, turning with arm movement to stage R. Repeat this 4 times, 4 walks to L. pause for sway of skirts, front line move down stage. ALL exit, with 4 walks step and curtsey, front line starting with L. foot, back line with R. Repeat this 3 times with 4 walks finishing facing front, turn upstage, walking off with partners.
No. 11. FINALE ACT I.	MEN and GIRLS enter from all sides, taking positions round tree outside Inn, grouping in twos-threes. ALL remain in positions until Duet CHARTERIS and MATHILDE. All curtsey as couple walk round stage, 6 DANCERS skip round couple, reversing, then pair off to join in jig. ALL VILLAGERS skip round in twos-threes, making chain movement ALL ending in positions round tree. QUAKERS enter stage R. in two lines as VILLAGERS run to other positions. Stage L. CHORUS react at " Ah !' Paree " Number, GIRLS make circle round tree to Refrain, taking original positions for Finale. At Curtain, VILLAGERS on bench outside Inn, standing on tree seat ; QUAKERS on stage R., all face upstage at exit of PRUDENCE.
No. 12. OPENING ACT II. *Movements* :	Curtain rises on 12 GIRL SINGERS, 6 DANCERS. 2 GIRLS sitting on seat either side back stage, 2 seated at tables in front, 2 standing behind, OTHERS grouped. TOINETTE C. DANCERS take positions 2 each side and 2 C. DANCING GIRLS commence with R. foot movement from side to side, turning to arabesque position. Repeat twice. Commence with L. foot 2 walks and sway, turning to front. Repeat step on R. foot to commence Dance. For Dance : L. kick up to front, back 1 turn, 4 movements commencing with R. foot, finishing with arabesque turn. Repeat turn twice L. kick reverse movement. Repeat, 4 walks to C. around TOINETTE. On Refrain GIRLS move to positions C. as MADAME BLUM goes C. SINGERS exit L. DANCERS exit with curtsey to R.
No. 13. "THEREABOUTS."	DANCERS enter 3 R. side, 3 L. with walks to positions (4 front C. 2 back stage) swaying to commencement of Dance Routine.

No. 16. "COME TO THE BALL."	12 Couples. Introduction Music couples walk 4 abreast through swing door downstage to C. pausing, turning R. and L., walking round to positions forming semi-circle. 6 MANNEQUINS enter through double doors U.C. on music cue "So let's celebrate," walk downstage in twos, turning L. and R., meeting in straight line, walking forward and turning to show off costumes, ALL turning upstage walking slowly, 3 MANNEQUINS turn back to walk downstage front. ALL walk round in circle, finishing 3 on each corner of stage. CHORUS remain in position during dialogue between PRINCE and PRUDENCE at end of MANNEQUINS' walk, until PRINCE'S cue "Tonight at the Ball." At start of Song DANCERS and MANNEQUINS stage R. and L. walk up to PRINCE C. stand and sway and then face him, each in turn either side, bend and look back as they pass to original positions, then kneel. PRINCE turns to R. and as he does this GIRLS get up and kneel again. He turns to GIRLS L. and they stand and kneel again in positions. At music cue "Come in your beauty" GIRLS leave partners, coming forward to form a line either side of PRINCE behind MANNEQUINS, who are still kneeling, each in turn bends and looks back at PRINCE as she stands behind MANNEQUINS with her male partner. At music cue "I will be loyal" MANNEQUINS move upstage with 4 movements, taking arms side to side making semicircle. On cue "Hailing as Queens of the Ball" ALL curtsey, SINGERS moving forward as MANNEQUINS in line do waltz movements to L. and R., sway L. to R., turn and repeat, 3 walking to R. corner, 3 to L. corner. PRINCE C. finishes Refrain. Repeat Refrain with full CHORUS : couples face front, MEN on inside, take GIRLS' hands as they move forward and back to a waltz movement 3 times, MANNEQUINS at the same time crossing over the PRINCE in turn from either side, first stage L. then R., finishing with 3 either side of PRINCE with waltz step, facing each corner of stage. Turning all upstage MANNEQUINS kneel in twos with PRINCE C. ALL looking up, MEN bow, GIRLS curtsey. For Encore Refrain GIRLS and MEN walk upstage from sides off stage R. and L. MANNEQUINS cross over with PRINCE, turn into circle, walking in two lines of 3, PRINCE C. MANNEQUINS exit, 3 stage R. and 3 L. walking backwards. PRINCE finishes Number and exits through gates.
No. 17. "A DANCING LESSON."	TONY and PRUDENCE C. TONY shows PRUDENCE how to "Take a step" with 3 steps back, lifting his R. foot. He repeats this twice, moving slightly to stage L. holding PRUDENCE by the hand. BOTH together do Polka step to stage L. PRUDENCE steps on TONY'S foot, as she does this she turns round and TONY leads her back to C. BOTH move to stage L. with waltz movement (PRUDENCE counting 1, 2 3) and over to stage R. TONY catches

	PRUDENCE in his arms, taking her to C. He waltzes her round stage, taking both her hands and finishing C. On " I'm really learning how it's done " PRUDENCE runs to stage R. TONY, standing C. sings " If it does not weary you once more we'll take it through," they join hands C. and commence waltz backwards and forwards and into waltz movement round stage. On " I am sure to make a blunder " PRUDENCE comes downstage R. TONY pirouettes to stage L. and repeats this as PRUDENCE stands in position R. looking at him. On " Now I'd like to try it once more " TONY and PRUDENCE join hands C., waltz round stage to front. PRUDENCE R. TONY L. both turn waltzing and meet C. TONY takes PRUDENCE as she pirouettes round stage, finishing with spin and curtsey upstage C. Exit with polka step both together round stage and run off to R.1.E.
No. 18. "BARBIZON."	BLUM, PHOEBE, CHARTERIS, MATHILDE. 16 marching steps all in line front stage. 16 marching steps back in line. On " I give my wages," ALL sway L. to R. 8 times, turning into C. on " It would be good." Turn to R., march until " Happy time will go," turn, march back to " Chanticleer will crow." Pas-de-Bouree movement commencing on R. foot 4 times. Box movement. GIRLS forward on R. Men back on L. GIRLS 4 steps to L. of stage. MEN 4 steps to R. of stage. ALL turn into one line. At " Smartest to catch an artist," ALL face front marching until " Tumble in the hay " ALL face in C. L.R. turn, march upstage singing " Barbizon," turning on " We'll have a cottage," march down front. For Dance 4 steps marching on spot, turn to R., 4 steps marching on spot, face front, 4 steps marching to front and turning L. R. turn upstage for 8 marching steps, back down front and exit R.
No. 19. FINALE ACT II.	WORK GIRLS standing at tables R. Enter CHARTERIS and PHOEBE R.2.E. Ensemble : Enter R. and L. 2 DANCERS move with MATHILDE and TOINETTE across stage to L. corner, giving names to LAROSE. Couples (MAN and GIRL) stand round stage. During dialogue PHOEBE and JEREMIAH exit through gates singing " Rule Britannia." At music cue " Ha ! ha ! Monsieur Larose." WORK GIRLS, TOINETTE and MATHILDE march from stage L. to C., taking 8 steps and a curtsey pointing to LAROSE with R. hand, walking back to positions in corner stage L. CHORUS remain in position, 2 GIRLS on stage R. walk to C., taking 3 steps and a curtsey as CHORUS sing and return to original positions until Curtain.
No. 20. OPENING ACT III. CHAMPAGNE BALLET.	Sounds of laughter, talking, etc. and general revelry as Curtain rises on couples grouped round stage at tables R. and L. Chain movement round stage on introduction music. Enter DANCERS from R.I.E. dressed as WAITERS, they do short line routine on point finishing

No. 21. " COULEUR DE ROSE."	on stage. Singers applaud. DANCERS run off L. as PRINCIPAL DANCER enters R. and dances short modern Ballet. SINGERS applaud. DANCERS re-enter and remain in position, ALL rising and bowing as PRINCE enters up L. PRINCE C. seated on table. On Refrain couples sway. On second Refrain ensemble sing as 6 COULEUR-DE-ROSE GIRLS waltz round stage in circle with PRINCE C., TOINETTE and DIANE waltzing up and down stage turning and finishing in curtsey. ALL exit on line " Man with the limp."
No. 22. " Mr. JEREMIAH, ESQUIRE."	PHOEBE and JEREMIAH do 2 Schottische steps. Music changes tempo and they do comedy waltz round stage. PHOEBE pulls JEREMIAH to C. and exits walking close together singing last 16 bars.
No. 23. " TONY FROM AMERICA."	6 DANCERS enter from stage R. forming semi-circle, 8 turns, 2 pas-de-Bouree reverses, kick into circle, ALL kneeling, waltzing back into line, movement forward and back circular kick to front. Exit in line stage R.

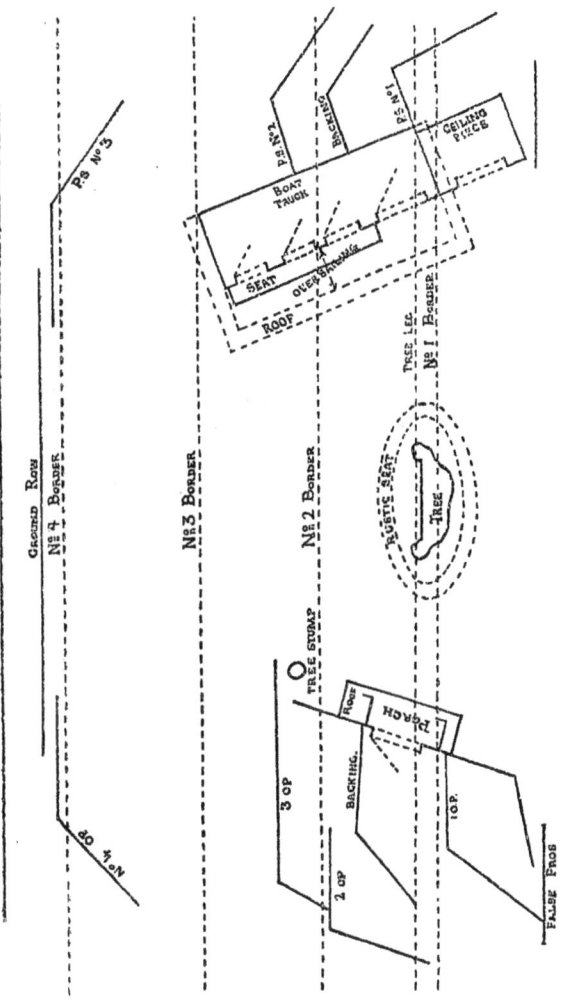

ACT I. A corner in a picturesque old world English village on a June morning. The Backcloth represents the landscape with hay ricks R. and a stream running from L. to foreground and under an old wide stone bridge on R. which leads from R.U.E. to R.C. of stage. The church is not visible. A Tree Wing masks R.3.E., and below this is the Quakers' Dwelling which extends to R.1.E., where there is the front door. Entrance at R.I.E. below House. At L.U.E. is a Tree Wing and L.3.E. is Entrance to the Inn Yard. C. is a Set Tree, the trunk surrounded by a wooden seat, the trunk wide enough to conceal two persons sitting behind it. At L.1.E. is an Arbour Entrance as though leading to a Bowling Green. The Borders are foliage to match the Tree Wings.

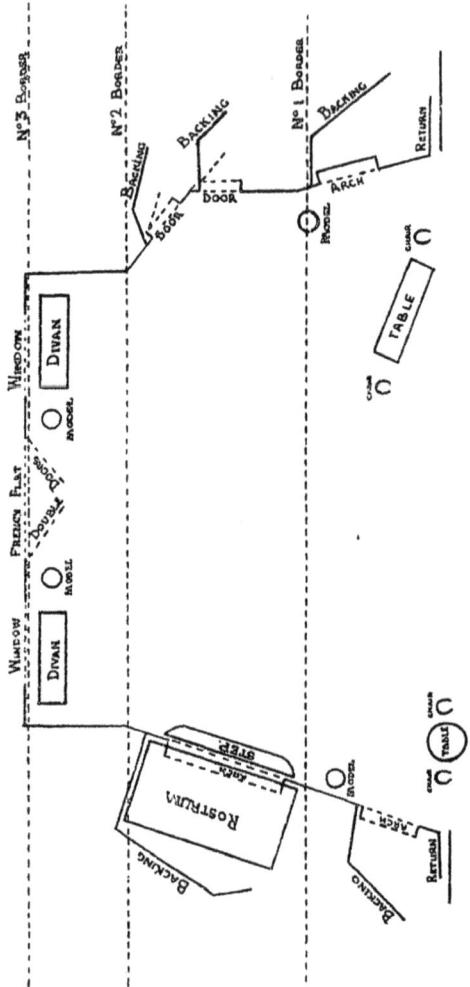

ACT II. The Reception Room at La Maison Blum, Paris. A spacious, artistically decorated apartment on the ground floor, looking on to one of the most fashionable shopping streets in Paris. At R.2 is an arched opening fitted with elegant curtains. At C. is a double door forming the Entrance from the street. At L.2. are two doors to fitting rooms. The upper one fitted with lock and large key. At R.1. and L.1. are arched openings with curtains similar to those at R.3. Down R.C. is an oblong table and 2 chairs, on table are writing materials and a telephone. Down R. are a round white table and 2 white chairs. 2 satin covered divans, 1 under grilled windows, R. and L. of doors at back. 4 modern stands draped with crepe silk, 1 L, 1 R., above L. and R.1.E, 1 on each side of doors C.

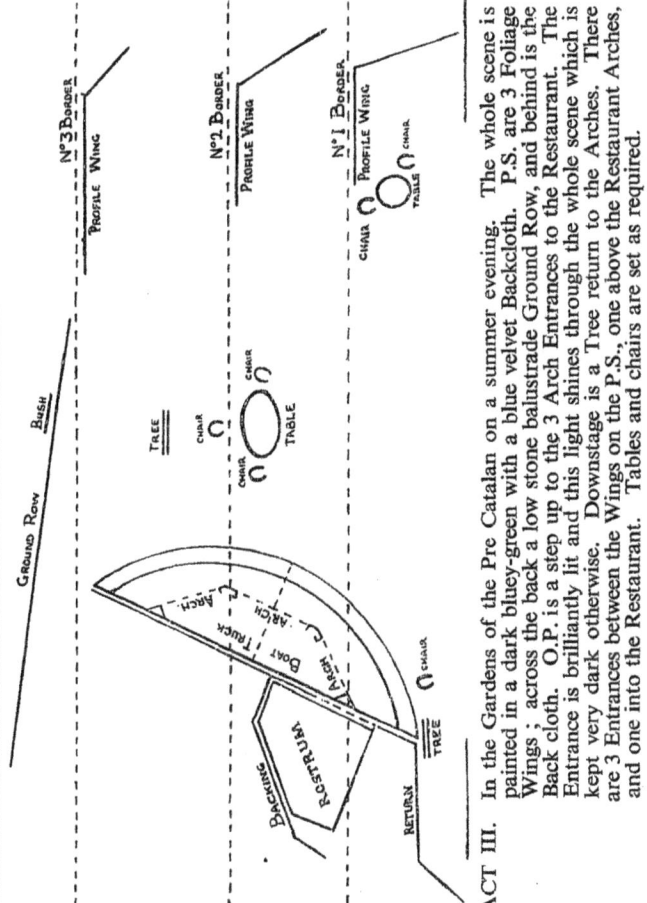

ACT III. In the Gardens of the Pre Catalan on a summer evening. The whole scene is painted in a dark bluey-green with a blue velvet Backcloth. P.S. are 3 Foliage Wings ; across the back a low stone balustrade Ground Row, and behind is the Back cloth. O.P. is a step up to the 3 Arch Entrances to the Restaurant. The Entrance is brilliantly lit and this light shines through the whole scene which is kept very dark otherwise. Downstage is a Tree return to the Arches. There are 3 Entrances between the Wings on the P.S., one above the Restaurant Arches, and one into the Restaurant. Tables and chairs are set as required.

PROPERTY PLOT

ACT I.

ON STAGE :

RIGHT OF STAGE :	1 Wooden Seat or Form (Bench for Inn).
CENTRE :	1 Tree Stump.
LEFT OF STAGE :	1 Round Wooden Seat for Tree in 2 Sections.

OFF STAGE :

RIGHT :
- 15 Prayer Books for QUAKERS.
- 1 Prayer Book for PRUDENCE
- 1 Town Crier Bell.
- 1 Servant's Tin Trunk
- 2 Baskets of Rose Petals.
- 1 Broken Bell Rope.
- 4 Parcels for TONY.
- 1 Woolly Lamb.

LEFT :
- 1 Trestle Table for wedding breakfast.
- 12 Wooden Mugs.
- 2 Wooden Trays.
- 8 Champagne Glasses (Silver plate).
- 3 Champagne Bottles.
- 8 Table Napkins.
- 2 White Table Cloths.
- 2 Dishes of Fruit.
- 2 Plates of Sandwiches.
- 1 Glass Water Jug.
- 1 Wine Decanter.
- 4 Green Chairs.

PERSONAL HAND PROPS :
- 1 Ruby Brooch in case for TONY.
- 1 Marriage Certificate for CHARTERIS.
- 1 Red Handkerchief for WILLIAM.
- 1 Handbag for MADAME BLUM.
- Cigars for JEREMIAH.

ACT II.

ON STAGE :	3 White Tables. 4 White Chairs. 4 Milliners' Stands with 4 Dress Lengths (Red Green Yellow Grey). 2 Settees with 2 Satin Covers.
RIGHT OF STAGE :	Key for Trick Door (set on Table). 1 White Vase with Bowl of Flowers (set in Alcove).
LEFT OF STAGE :	1 Telephone 1 Ash Tray 1 Writing Pad 1 Tape Measure (Set on Table) Letters Millinery Oddments
OFF STAGE :	
RIGHT :	1 Bell 10 White Handbags for LADIES. 1 Chocolate Box with Red Ribbon. 2 Lady's Garters Red and Blue. 1 Packet of Letters tied with Red Ribbon.
LEFT :	10 White Handbags for LADIES. 1 Nosegay for PHOEBE. 1 White Flower Bowl with Flowers.
PERSONAL HAND PROPS :	14 Race Glasses for MEN. 14 Walking Sticks for MEN. 1 Walking Stick for TONY 1 Walking Stick for PRINCE. 1 White Dress Glove for JEREMIAH. 1 Warrant for LAROSE. Small Bags for PRUDENCE (White and Coloured). Handbag for DIANE containing Mirror and Powder Puff and Packet of Letters tied with Red Ribbon, and Packet of Letters tied with Blue Ribbon.

ACT III.

ON STAGE :	2 Green Tables (Garden Type) 6 Green Chairs. 2 Cocktail Coolers with Bottles.

LIGHTING PLOT

FRONT OF HOUSE.

ACT I.

Flood Stage to open.
No Spot on Mrs. LUKYN.
Flood for QUAKERS—keep off side legs.
1 Spot on PHOEBE—1 on MATHILDE—2 floods on PHOEBE'S exit.
Both spots on MATHILDE.
Spot on CHARTERIS at Bridge.
Spot on MADAME BLUM on Bridge.
Spot on TONY and CHARTERIS on Bridge.
Spot on NATHANIEL & RACHEL on Bridge.
Spot on JEREMIAH at entrance Quaker House.
Spot on PRUDENCE when she stops walking over Bridge.
3 Spots on PRUDENCE for number " A Quaker Girl."
Spot on CHARTERIS on Bridge.
Spot on MADAME BLUM at Inn door.
Spot on MATHILDE at Inn door.
Spot on Mrs. LUKYN & WILLIAM at Inn door.
Spot on PHOEBE on Bridge.
Spot on JEREMIAH at Arch down L.
4 Spots on JEREMIAH for Number. " Just as Father Used to do."
Spot on PHOEBE at Inn.
Spot on PRINCIPALS at Wedding Entrance.
Spot on PRINCIPALS all through Finale.

ACT II.

Flood to open.
Spot MADAME BLUM Centre Doors.
Spot LAROSE Centre Doors.
Spot MATHILDE R.U.E.
Spot PHOEBE L.1.E.
Spot JEREMIAH Centre Doors.
Spot DIANE & TONY Centre Doors.
Flood Chorus.
Spot PRINCE & PRUDENCE Centre Doors.
Spot MADAME BLUM L.1.E.
2 Spots on PRINCE for Number " Come to the Ball."
Spot TONY L.1.E.   PHOEBE R.2.E.   CHARTERIS R.1.E.
Spot MADAME BLUM R.2.E.
Spot PRUDENCE R.I.E.
Spot JEREMIAH Centre Doors.
Spot LAROSE Centre Doors.
Spot PHOEBE R.2.E.
Spot MATHILDE & CHARTERIS R.2.E.
Spot MADAME BLUM R.2.E.
Spot PHOEBE R.1.E.
Spot JEREMIAH R.2.E.
Spot PRINCE Centre Doors.
Spot TOINETTE R.2.E.
Spot TONY L.1.E.
Spot PRUDENCE R.2.E.

Spot TOINETTE L.3.E.
Spot JEREMIAH R.2.E.
Spot PHOEBE R.2.E.
Spot all PRINCIPALS during Finale.

ACT III.

Off to open.
Spot PRINCIPAL DANCER.   White through house piece.
Spot PRINCE L.2.E.   Change to 36 Pink for number.
Spot DIANE L.2.E.
Spot TOINETTE R.C.
Spot LAROSE L.2.E.
Spot MADAME BLUM.   DUHAMEL through house piece.
Spot PHOEBE R.C.
Spot JEREMIAH L.2.E.
2 Spots on PHOEBE & JEREMIAH for Number.   "Mr. Jeremiah Esquire."
Spot MATHILDE, PRUDENCE, CHARTERIS through house piece.
Spot PRINCE through house piece.
Spot MADAME BLUM through house piece.
Spot DUHAMEL R.2.E.
Flood stage, 32 Blue with two arcs.
Spot one White and one 18 Blue on PRUDENCE for Number.
   "Tony from America."
Spot TONY R.C. on entrance.
Spot PRINCIPALS as they enter for Finale.
Flood stage 18 Blue for Finale line up.
Remain on till final curtain.
Never Flood White in this Act. After the PRINCIPALS have all come down and when they have finished singing "Tony from America"—shutter in to catch them 18 Blue.

STAGE.

ACT I.

Full Up. Amber and White Circuits and Floats.
Stage Floods R. ; Floods White in all Entrances.
One Flood behind No. 1, wing shining up on Quaker House.
Stage Floods L. ; Floods White all Entrances.
One White Strip inside Inn *on floor* under window.
No Checks in this Act.

ACT II.

Full Up. All White Circuits and Floats.
1 Tower R. ; 1 Tower L. White, behind French Flat against Backcloth.
1 Flood in each Entrance L. and R. Open White.
One check down at cue battens and floats to quarter.
Stage Floods and Towers remain at full.
At Cue, Quick Full Up on Switchboard wheel.

ACT III.

Battens. Blue 32. Floats Blue 32 Full.
Stage R. One Spot. Four Amber shining on to Stage Centre through Restaurant window. Two Flood at Half White shining down on stage through Restaurant. No Checks during Act.

DRESS PLOT

Tony . . Act 1. White Suit, Brown and White Shoes, White Felt Hat, Cream Shirt with Collar attached, White Socks, Navy Tie.

Act 2. Black Morning Coat, Striped Trousers, Grey Waistcoat, Black Shoes, White Shirt, Turn-down Stiff Collar, Grey Tie, Grey Top Hat.

Act 3. Dress Suit, White Shirt, Collar, Tie, Black Silk Hat.

Capt. Charteris Act. 1. Black Morning Coat, Striped Trousers, Dress Shirt, Fawn Waistcoat, Turn-down Collar, Grey Tie, Socks, Soft Black Felt Hat, Shoes.

Act. 2. Blue Striped Coat and Trousers, Waistcoat, Blue check Shirt—Collar attached, Blue Tie, Double Shoes.

Act 3. Evening Coat and Trousers, White Waistcoat, White Tie, Double Shirt Act 1. Collar.

Jeremiah . . Act 1. Quaker Hat, Wig, (Worn throughout) Black Coat with White Collar and Cuffs, Black Trousers, Grey Waistcoat, Black Bow, Black Stockings, Black buckle Shoes.

Act 2. Check Suit, Yellow Waistcoat, White Shirt, Turn-down Collar, White and Green Stockings, Brown Shoes, Grey Bowler Hat, Green Tie.

Act 3. Blue Coat, Blue Trousers, Red Waistcoat, Black Shoes, White Socks, Dress Shirt, Blue Tie, Turn-down Collar.

Prince Carlo . Act 2. Morning Coat, Striped Trousers, Fawn Waistcoat, Star and Red and Mauve Ribbon, Dress Shirt, Turn-down Collar, Black Socks, Black Shoes, Grey Top Hat.

Act 3. Dress Suit, Double Shirt Act 2, Wing Collar, White Tie, Jewelled Order, Double Shoes and Socks.

Nathaniel Pym . Act 1. Black Coat, Collar and Cuffs attached, Breeches, Quaker Hat, Buckle Shoes, Black Stockings.

Act 2. As Chorus Men.

1st Gendarme . Act 2. Navy Coat and Trousers, Navy Cloak, Peaked Hat, Sword and Sword Belt.

Act 3. White Trousers, White Tunic, White Hood and Mask.

2nd GENDARME	Act 2.	Navy Coat and Trousers, Navy Cloak, Peaked Cap, Sword and Sword Belt.
JARGE	Act 1.	Straw Hat, Smock, Boots, Gaiters, Trousers, Beard. Black Tail Coat and Trousers, Brown Velvet Waistcoat, Dickey, Collar, Bow, Felt Hat.
LAROSE	Act 2.	Black Frock Coat and Trousers, Grey Waistcoat, Shirt, Wing Collar, Cravat, Grey Gloves, Black Shoes. Blue Smock, Black Bow, Purple Beret, Velvet Trousers.
	Act 3.	Blue Cloak, Blue Hat, Beard (Silk) Double Trousers and Shirt Act 2.
DUHAMEL	Act 2.	Morning Coat, Grey Trousers, Dress Shirt, Wing Collar, Yellow Gloves, Grey Cravat, Crook Stick, Black Silk Top Hat, Black Shoes, Socks.
	Act 3.	Blue Order, Ribbon and Riband, Dress Suit, Double linen and Shoes.
WILLIAM	Act 1.	Old Evening Suit, Black Waistcoat, 2 Cloths, Black Shoes and Socks, Dress Shirt, Turn-over Collar, Black Bow.
PRUDENCE	Act 1.	Grey Linen Quaker Dress, with Collar, Cuffs and Apron attached, White Bonnet, White Stockings, Black Shoes, White Mittens.
	Act 2.	Grey Chiffon Dress, with Collar, Cuffs and Apron attached, Grey Ballet Shoes, Double Mittens Act 1, White Organdie Bonnet. Blue Net Dress, Blue Net and Silver Headdress and Veil, Blue Shoes, Blue Handbag.
	Act 3.	Blue Chiffon Dress, Pink Lace Collar, Cuffs and Apron, Lace Bonnet, Blue Mittens. Blue Bag, Pink Ballet Shoes.
PRINCESS MATHILDE	Act 1.	Green Lace Dress embroidered White, White Picture Hat, Green Satin Sandals. White Wedding Dress, White Veil and Headdress, Silver Shoes.
	Act 2.	Blue Checked Dress with Black Apron and Pincushion attached, Tape Measure. Frilly Petticoat attached, Frilly Knickers, Cerise Bow, Black Strap Shoes.
	Act 3.	Turquoise Blue Net Dress, Navy Blue Net Cape and Hood, Silver Shoes.
MADAME BLUM	Act 1.	Black Jumper and Skirt (rimmed seecoloid), Black and Flame Turban, Long Black Gloves, Diamond Brooch, Stockings, Black Shoes, Black Handbag.

	Act 2. Black Sequin Tunic, Black Skirt trimmed with Sequins, Coloured Sequin Turban, Short Black Suede Gloves, Diamond Clips, Double Black Shoes Act 1.
	Act 3. Patterned Chiffon Dress trimmed Sequins, Black and Sequin Headdress, Double Clips, Suede Shoes.

PHOEBE — Act 1. Black Taffeta Dress with White Apron, Collar and Cuffs, Black Bow, Frilly Petticoat and Knickers, Black Shoes.
Act 2. Double Act 1.
Act 3. Blue Taffeta Dress with White Collar, Cuffs, Apron and Petticoat, Carnival Hat, Double Knickers, Blue Shoes and Shoe Bows.

TOINETTE — Act 2. Black Velvet Dress, Black high-heeled Shoes, Black Brassiere, Black Pants.
Act 3. Yellow Ballet Dress, Net Bow for hair, Ballet Shoes.

DIANE — Act 2. Cerise, Red and Mauve long Dress, Mauve Net Picture Hat, Mauve long Gloves, Cerise Bag, Silver Shoes, Dress Clips, and Earrings.
Act 3. Green Dress, embroidered Gold Sequins, Gold Sequin Feather and Green Net Headdress, Double Shoes and Jewellery.

Mrs. LUKYN — Blue Alpaca Dress with Collar and Cuffs, Black Apron, Black Shoes, Black Stockings. Spectacles, 2 keys, False Hair front and coil

RACHEL PYM — Brown Linen Dress, with Collar, Cuffs and Apron, White Bonnet, Black Shoes, White Stockings.

CHORUS MEN — Act 1. Half are dressed as Villagers, in Breeches, Smocks, Gaiters, etc. Half are dressed as Quakers.
Act 2. All are dressed in Grey Morning Coats, Trousers, Top Hats, Field Glasses, Canes, etc.
Act 3. All are dressed in Carnival Costumes.

CHORUS GIRLS SINGERS — Act 1. All are dressed as Quakers.
Act 2. All are dressed in Long Dresses, with full Skirts, short sleeves, long Gloves and big Picture Hats.
Act 3. All are in various Carnival Costumes.

DANCERS :	Act 1.	Village Maidens in various coloured Skirts, contrasting Blouses, White Aprons, Straw Hats, Bonnets, etc.
	Act 2.	Two Girls are dressed as Pages in Turquoise Dresses and Hats. These Girls open the big doors at the back of the set.
		The Others are dressed as Work Girls to Mme Blum. They are in short Blue Check Dresses, Black Aprons, with Pin-cushions, Tape Measures, and Cerise Bows in their hair.
	Act 3.	The Girls open as Waiters, in Blue Tights and Blue Velvet Tail Coats, White Stiff Shirts and Men's Wigs.
		They change into Couleur de rose Dresses. Long White Ballet Dresses with Pink Feather Headdresses.
		They change again into Long Blue Classical Ballet Dresses for Number " Tony from America."

www.ingramcontent.com/pod-product-compliance
Ingram Content Group UK Ltd.
Pitfield, Milton Keynes, MK11 3LW, UK
UKHW021918060225

454771UK00026B/659